Who am I really?

W9-BHX-460

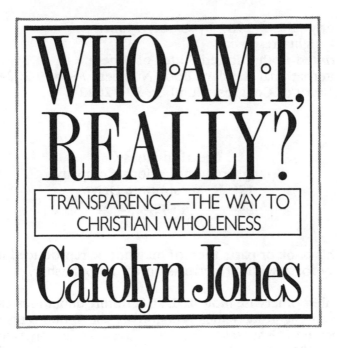

WHO∘AM∘I, REALLY?

TRANSPARENCY—THE WAY TO CHRISTIAN WHOLENESS

Carolyn Jones

Creation House
Altamonte Springs, Florida

Copyright © 1987 by Carolyn Jones
All rights reserved.
Printed in the United States of America.
International Standard Book Number: 0-88419-202-4
Library of Congress Number: 87-72022

Creation House
Strang Communications Company
190 N. Westmonte Drive
Altamonte Springs, FL 32714
(305) 869-5005

This book or parts thereof may not be reproduced in any form without permission of the publisher.

Unless otherwise indicated, all Scripture quotations are from the King James Version of the Bible. Verses marked TLB are taken from The Living Bible, copyright © 1971 by Tyndale House Publishers, Wheaton, Illinois. Used by permission. Verses marked NIV are taken from the New International Version of the Bible.

Permission was granted to excerpt from the following:

"I Am Loved" by William J. and Gloria Gaither. Copyright © 1978 by William J. Gaither. All rights reserved. Used by permission. "The Warrior Is a Child" by Twila Paris. Copyright © 1984 by Singspiration Music/ASCAP. All rights reserved. Used by permission of the Benson Company, Inc., Nashville, Tennessee. *The Art of Understanding Yourself* by Cecil Osborne. Copyright © 1967 by The Zondervan Publishing House. Used by permission. *Dropping Your Guard* by Charles Swindoll. Copyright © 1983 by Word Books. Used by permission.

Contents

With grateful appreciation to my husband, John, who has believed in me, encouraged me to respond to God's leading in my life and promoted this effort.

A special thank-you to Jan White and Evelyn Bence who helped me shape and refine this book.

PART I

TRANSPARENCY:

Opening the Door To Who I Really Am

ONE

Transparent in A World of Masks

S everal years ago we returned home from a family vacation to discover that the pump on our well was broken. We had no running water in our house, and, on top of that, the air conditioning in my car wasn't cooling.

But, despite problems, life goes on. Our pets—a Lassie-looking collie, an old-lady overstuffed dachshund, a feisty miniature dachshund and a beautiful, fluffy, black and white cat—had an appointment at the veterinarian for their vaccinations.

On a hot August day, I loaded two kids, one baby, three dogs and one cat into my car. Of course the air conditioning didn't work, but we had to keep the car windows rolled up so the animals wouldn't jump out. By the time we got to the vet's office, we were sweaty, tired and a little unnerved.

"You certainly have your hands full," the veterinarian observed as he walked into the tiny cubicle where the children, the animals and I waited for him.

Exasperated, I explained my story and asked, "Could I just leave these animals here? I'll call my husband and he can pick them up on his way home for lunch."

"Fine," he said. At that point, he probably wouldn't have dared to refuse my request.

When I got home, I phoned John's office and asked him to pick up the animals at the vet. He said he would, although he'd be later than usual as he had an appointment at a nearby naval base before coming home for lunch. (John is an attorney who also serves as a lieutenant commander in the navy reserve.)

When John walked in the house, Jacket, our tan and white collie, bounded in, characteristically slurping all over everything. Then a dachshund ran in, stopped in front of me and pooped on the carpet!

"John, that's not Missy!" I exclaimed.

Cool as can be, he responded, "What do you mean that's not Missy? Didn't you say she'd lost weight while we were on vacation?"

"John, that dog isn't half as big as Missy, and besides she's got a wart on her nose."

He seemed to have a one-track mind. "What do you mean that's not Missy? We've had her for 17 years. I know what she looks like."

I vehemently reaffirmed that that dog was not

6

our Missy and asked the question taking shape in my. mind, "Where's Scamper?"

John, still thinking he was Johnny-on-the-spot, replied, "The cat jumped out of the car. He's in the garage." That didn't seem unusual to me, and I centered my concern back on Missy. She was older than all our children; she was like a member of the family.

I called the vet's office. "Excuse me, this is Carolyn Jones. My husband has brought home the wrong dog."

"No, no, no, Mrs. Jones," the doctor's assistant insisted. "I've worked here for fourteen years and we've never made a mistake like that." I insisted; the dog I was looking at was not mine.

She laid the phone down and went to check on it. After a few minutes, she picked up the receiver and hesitantly said, "Mrs. Jones, I'm so sorry. We have your dog here...and we also have your cat."

"Well, what cat do I have?" I questioned, trying hard to keep my cool.

"You have a cat named Felix who's prone to scratch and a dog named Oscar," she explained.

I hung up the phone and exploded with the news. "That must be the reason the dog and cat started fighting in the car," John said sheepishly. Then he added, "And I backed into a car in the parking lot leaving the vet's."

We went out to the garage to look for Felix. The cat had jumped up under the fender of the car and was sitting on top of the tire out of our reach. Now John had his white military uniform on and there he was, lying on the greasy garage floor, calling,

"Here, kitty, here, kitty." The cat wouldn't budge.

By this time John was as upset as I. He began walking around in circles, throwing up his hands and exclaiming, "I'm an attorney. I'm supposed to work for a living and all I'm doing is running *your* errands!" The fruit of the Spirit, patience and temperance, to name a few, went flying out the window. Finally we called the vet who sent an animal rescuer to get the cat and dog.

But there was still one problem. The melee had held John up; at the office, a client had been waiting for him for an hour. This woman had just about exhausted her patience. When John walked in the office, she demanded, "Mr. Jones, where have you been?"

John could have done one of two things at that moment. He could have done what most of us would and said, "I'm very sorry. I apologize for being late." That would have been the end of it.

But, praise God, he dared to be vulnerably honest. "Sit down. You're not going to believe this," he said to the client and the office staff.

By the time he finished telling the story, everyone was crying from laughing so hard. He then ushered the client into his private office. When she sat down, she made a startling statement: "Mr. Jones, when I came here, I thought my plans were set. I was going to meet with you and then go home and end my life. But I've changed my mind. If you can go through something like that and make me laugh for the first time in nine months, maybe there is hope."

The Big Cover-up

Too often we hide our feelings and circumstances from others. We feel safer behind our masks. In his book *The Trauma of Transparency*, J. Grant Howard teaches about masks.

Many terms are used to depict this tendency we all have to hide from one another. We cover up our needs. We bury our thoughts. We repress our feelings. We mull things over inwardly. We are quiet, reserved or even withdrawn. We are introverted. Sullen. Pouting. Shy. Bashful. We say, "I couldn't care less," but we really do. We say, "Leave me alone," because we don't want anyone to step inside and see what really is happening.

We say, "I don't want to talk about it," even though we desperately need to. We say, "Nothing is bothering me," when in all honesty a problem is clawing our soul to shreds. We say, "I can work this out myself," when in reality we can't; we need help.[1]

When John and I married in August 1965 after graduating from Florida State University, we knew all about wearing masks. That fall he enrolled in law school; we quickly learned how to be the "perfect American couple." We would fuss like cats and dogs all the way to a social gathering. Then we'd walk inside, put on our masks—all smiles and friendly chatter. After proving to ourselves and everyone else that we were among the most popular couples there, we would walk out and fuss like cats and dogs all the way home. I think we were among the world's best mask wearers.

I once read the Greek myth about Narcissus. According to the legend, he stared at his image in a reflecting pool until he died. His gaze was so transfixed by that image of himself that even in death he longed for another glimpse.

My first thought was, My goodness, what a story of vanity. Then I began to wonder if the legend really had more to do with focusing all one's attention on one's image than with vanity. Often people focus their attention on living up to an image of themselves; they hide the real self behind a mask.

Why do people wear masks? Because they've got something to hide: anger, rejection, insecurity, guilt. And they're too afraid or too proud to let other people see their human frailties.

Jesus doesn't intend for any of us to live that way. He came to free us, to give us abundant life, to lead us to a place where we don't need masks, where we can dare to be real and vulnerable with one another.

But our journey to that place of transparency is long and sometimes hard. Every person has to come to a place where he realizes that he is not the only one who carries the scars, who is less than perfect. Each person needs to share victories and defeats with fellow travelers.

The Benefits of Transparency

When we say how we feel, the other person will often say, "I feel that same way, and I thought I was the only one who suffered with that. You mean you've got a problem there, too?" When the masks come down, relationship happens. And Satan is defeated because he cannot keep us isolated and alone. Have you ever noticed that if you dare to be vulnerable with someone, that person will often respond with his struggles, even if it's in a different area.

I limit you when I hold up a mask and allow you to see only what I want you to see—that good, perfect, honest woman who's quite different from the one who's feeling wounded or weary or worrisome. You look at my mask and think, *She's a little better than I am. She probably wouldn't accept me if I told how I really feel.* Then you put on a mask to match mine. By wearing my mask I dictate to you that you have to wear yours. Now two people are isolated behind two separate walls. Both are acting and saying all the right things, but they are bleeding on the inside because nobody knows their true feelings.

Now please understand that I'm not saying that becoming transparent means we have to run to the nearest stranger on the street and say, "Let me tell you all the things in my life that are out of order."

I'm saying that everyone needs to understand who he is and what he is feeling. We need someone who loves us and accepts us as we are—someone we can go to and tell how we really feel.

Charles Swindoll says,

> The purpose of our journey is not simply to unmask and parade our pain as we expose the truth of who we are. The ultimate objective is to cultivate an atmosphere of such openness that we are free to share our dreams

in an unguarded manner, talk about hopes and hammer out goals for our lives. By becoming people who are comfortable to be around, we encourage the same thing in others.[2]

People like us better when we are honest and real. When Jack Hayford, the well-known California pastor, spoke at our church, John arranged for us to have dinner with him. If that's all I told you, you might be impressed that we went out to eat with such an outstanding minister. But if I told you that I was scared to death and tried to get out of it, you might identify with me and like me a little better; you might have felt the same way had you been in my place. You and I have a choice. We can either project what we want others to see, or we can be honest enough so others can identify with us.

Something happens when we dare to be vulnerable with each other. When the masks come down, and we express our feelings, the other person will find the freedom to express his feelings.

We're Only Human

"OK, everybody, masks off!" Charles Swindoll writes in his book *Dropping Your Guard*. He goes on to explain:

There are times when I want to stand up and make that announcement. I've never done it, but I sure have been tempted. Can you imagine the reaction? It would be a scary thing for most folks, especially those who have learned that survival comes a lot easier behind a mask.

There is a mask for whatever occasion. Have you noticed? No matter how you feel, regardless of the truth, if you become skilled at hiding behind your guard, you don't have to hassle with all the things that come with full disclosure. You feel safe. What you lack in honesty, you make up for in pseudo-security. If you wear an "I'm tough" mask, you don't have to worry about admitting how weak and frightened you actually are. If you keep your "I'm holy" mask in place, you never need to bother with people wondering if you struggle with spirituality.

Furthermore, the "I'm-cool-because-I've-got-it-all-together" mask comes in handy if you resist stuff like hard questions, vulnerable admissions, straight talk. Another familiar front is the "I'm-able-to-handle-all-this-pain-and-pressure" mask. No tears, not even a frown or hint of bewilderment is revealed. That one helps when you're surrounded by superpious folks who are impressed with answers like "Oh, I'm fine" and "I'm just claiming the victory," accompanied by eyelids at half mast and a nice appropriate smile.

The most tragic part of all is that the longer we do it, the better we get at it...and the more alone we remain in our hidden world of fear, pain, anger, insecurity, and grief—all those normal and natural emotions we hesitate to admit but that prove we are only human.[3]

WHO AM I REALLY?

Think about it: "All those normal and natural emotions we hesitate to admit...prove we are only human"—and God loves humans.

TWO

Knowing God

When you realize the enormity of God's love for you, you will trust Him enough to let Him look inside your life. Could you dare trust Him with who you are—the person behind the mask who has strengths and weaknesses? To overcome the fear or pride or insecurity that keeps us from being transparent before others, we must first accept God's love. We must trust Him with our imperfections so that He can use them and transform them to His good.

He Knows

Psalm 139 tells how well God knows us and how much He loves us.

O Lord, you have examined my heart and know everything about me. You know when I sit or stand. When far away you know my every thought. You chart the path ahead of me, and tell me where to stop and rest. Every moment, You know where I am. You know what I am going to say before I even say it. You both precede and follow me, and place your hand of blessing on my head.

This is too glorious, too wonderful to believe! I can *never* be lost to your Spirit! I can *never* get away from God! If I go up to heaven, you are there; if I go down to the place of the dead, you are there. If I ride the morning winds to the farthest oceans, even there your hand will guide me, your strength will support me. If I try to hide in the darkness, the night becomes light around me. For even darkness cannot hide from God; to you the night shines as bright as day. Darkness and light are both alike to you.

You made all the delicate, inner parts of my body, and knit them together in my mother's womb. Thank you for making me so wonderfully complex! It is amazing to think about. Your workmanship is marvelous—and how well I know it. You were there while I was being formed in utter seclusion! You saw me before I was born and scheduled each day of my life before I began to breathe. Every day was recorded in your Book!

How precious it is, Lord, to realize that you are thinking about me constantly! I can't even count how many times a day your thoughts turn towards me. And when I waken in the morning, you are still thinking of me! (Ps.

139:1-18, TLB).

We think we keep ourselves so hidden, yet God knows us better than we know ourselves. God is reaching out to us, but we are afraid for Him to see the real us.

He Is Strong

I grew up in a Christian home and went to church every week. The minister preached a very social gospel—talking about feeding the poor and taking care of the sick, but not a whole lot about Jesus. Although I knew God loved me, I didn't know what it meant to be saved. God, in His love, kept reaching out to me even as I was growing up. As a young girl, I went to a retreat. At the last meeting, the speaker invited all who wanted to dedicate their lives to God to come forward.

From my seat, about three-fourths of the way back, I told God, "If I go up there and dedicate my life, I'll have to go to Africa." I didn't want to go to Africa, not at that point in my life.

I was sure that if you dedicated your life to the Lord you had to be a foreign missionary. What other way was there to serve Him? I watched all those people walking down the aisle to the front and thought, *Look at all the people from Florida who are going to Africa.* Even though I didn't understand, God kept reaching out to me.

For one of the closing sessions of those meetings, I was asked to read the Scripture. I had never been so scared in all my life. I rehearsed and rehearsed that passage. I believe I could say it backwards to you today. It was the story of the Pharisee and the sinner who went into the temple to pray.

I stood up and shook through the whole thing, but I said it perfectly. Not one mistake. I was so relieved when I finished reading. All I had to do then was announce the prayer. I concluded, "Now would you all please bow your words for a head of prayer." The whole place cracked up. I was so embarrassed—I thought it was the end of my life. Being vulnerable was not fun, and in my embarrassing moment of weakness, I promised myself I'd never speak in front of a group again. Years later, when I began finding out who He is and who I am, God used two scriptures to teach me a lesson about strengths and weaknesses.

Second Corinthians 12:9 reads, "He said unto me, My grace is sufficient for thee: for My strength is made perfect in weakness." God's words were, "My strength is made perfect in weakness." That one little line started to change my life.

Then a phrase in Hebrews 11, the great faith chapter, just about knocked my socks off. The whole chapter is built around all the marvelous, wonderful deeds that people did for God—the faith, the strength, the character, the mighty acts that they accomplished. It just goes on and on extolling these people whom God used. Toward the middle of the chapter it says, "Who through faith subdued kingdoms, wrought righteousness, obtained promises, stopped the mouths of lions, quenched the violence of fire, escaped the edge of the sword...." And there in the midst of all that *strength* it continues, "...out of weakness were made strong" (vv. 33,34).

God taught me that transparency comes when you are so weak that His strength shines through you. He can't use you in your own strength. But when you say, "God, I am weak. I cannot do it," then you allow His strength to come through like a shining light.

Many people who minister to others project an aura of strength. They're not willing for anyone to see their weaknesses. They never let anyone see into their own lives. So the person hurting thinks the person ministering to them has no problems.

When we dare to minister out of our weakness, we can say, "I understand how you feel because I've been there. I accept you the way you are."

In his book *Loving God*, Chuck Colson talks about all his degrees and all his honors. He had prestige. He had fame. He had money. He had everything the world would admire, and yet God chose to use Chuck's time in prison to show him that he was to minister to prisoners. God didn't use Chuck's strength but his weakness, and now Chuck Colson's prison ministry is known around the world.

God is no respecter of persons. He is willing to use anyone who dares to be vulnerable. Remember, when we are weak, His strength shines through us.

He Is Love

I got a glimpse of this kind of love last summer when we went to the beach. A couple of families— good friends—were with us. While we were at a pool near the ocean, my younger son, Andrew, approached a teenage boy from one of the families. Andrew asked this tall, muscular young

19

man to take him to the beach.

From poolside, I watched these two in the water. The older boy would pick up my little freckle-faced son to keep him from getting hit by the waves; the older helped the younger dig in the sand; the two related on Andrew's level. I watched a unique relationship begin. A trust level was formed through a bonding that both felt.

This year when we were getting ready to go to the beach with the same friends, Andrew said to me, "Mom, when we get to the beach, I want to play with that boy." He hesitated a moment try-ing to remember the teenager's name, then he added, "You know, Mom, the one who likes me so much."

That's exactly what God wants for us. He wants us to get to the place with Him where we say, "God, I trust you with this. I trust You and open up myself to You because I know You're the one who likes me so much."

It's like the Bill Gaither song, "I am loved. You are loved. I can risk loving you, for the one who knows me best loves me most."[1] Now isn't that incredible? God, who knows even those areas of our lives that we have not looked at, loves us more than anyone.

Sometimes, we feel we have to be *good* before we come to God. But that is a waste of time, as we don't ever get good enough to come to God. He has described our righteousness as filthy rags. The apostle Paul certainly wasn't good enough. God had to knock him off a donkey to get his at-tention. Peter, who had walked with Jesus for three years and witnessed the miraculous, denied Him three times. But when these men put God first, He turned their lives around and used them mightily in ministry.

So many people have been taught that good works make you good enough for God. If that were true, a precious woman I know would be the first one at heaven's gate. Yet she doesn't know God.

God wants us to come to Him just as we are, with childlike trust. We don't have to prove anything to Him. Jesus taught that those who enter into the kingdom of God must do so like a little child. And those who come with the open arms of a child can enjoy a relationship with a loving Father who wants the best for us.

He Is Personal

God wants this kind of relationship with us. Yet it seems so difficult for some of us to accept the fact that God desires open communication with us. He wants to speak to us personally.

In *The Trauma of Transparency*, J. Grant Howard talks about the kind of relationship he desires to have: "I need a relationship with a person from whom I cannot hide. I need a relationship with a person at whom I can hurl, but who gives me no cause to and won't be alienated if I do it. I need a relationship with a person who will always tell me the truth."[2] Only in God can we find the kind of relationship we need and that's the kind of relationship He desires to give us.

Sometimes I wake up in the middle of the night and hear the Holy Spirit speaking to me, communicating through my innermost thoughts. Lying in the warmth and comfort of my bed, I've listened with intentions of writing it all down the next morning. But I've learned that I don't remember the thoughts unless I scribble them immediately. In fact, if I don't get out of bed and write them on paper, I toss and turn the rest of the night. I've even placed a little bench in the bedroom closet. There I keep a notepad and pencil for writing these thoughts.

One night, though, John, our three children and I were sleeping in a motel room when I awoke about 3 a.m. I started talking to God and listening for what He might want me to hear. In order not to disturb my husband and children, I decided there was only one place I could write. Closing the bathroom door, I switched on the light.

In the solitude of that bathroom, God taught me a lesson about how much He wants to communicate with us. He reminded me that the people in Old Testament times could not communicate with Him directly. The high priest entered the temple periodically to offer sacrifices. The sacrifices atoned for the people's sins. Then the priest came out and told everybody what God had to say.

God made sure I understood this Old Testament form of communication before He reminded me that, when Jesus died, the veil enclosing the holy of holies at the temple was torn in two. The veil was torn to symbolize that our relationship with the Father could be direct. After Jesus' death, the high priest didn't have to relay God's messages to us. We could communicate with Him ourselves.

"Yes, Lord," I replied. "I know all that. We've been taught that for a long time."

What came next startled me. He pointed out how most people today want "Old Testament Christianity." He directed His message to every Christian: "You want to sit in the pews and pay your dues, and let the high priest or person in the pulpit tell you what God has to say. It's easier than hearing from Him yourself."

God emphasized to me that Jesus sacrificed His life to establish this open relationship and communication for you and me with the Father. While it's necessary for the minister, priest or pastor to share God's Word and shepherd the flock, God wants to communicate with us personally.

For so many of us, Sunday morning services have become comfortable. We come to the sanctuary and praise God. We focus our attention on Him. We allow a glimmer of His light to shine on us on Sunday and live in darkness the rest of the week. It's easy to listen to the pastor's sermon and then forget about it Monday through Saturday.

By holding onto this type of Old Testament faith, we miss out on that moment-by-moment, one-to-one relationship with the living, loving God. It overwhelmed me to think God would give His only Son to provide direct communication between us and Him.

As I climbed back into bed and laid my head on the pillow, a scripture came to my mind. Permit me to paraphrase. Jesus asked Peter, "Who am I?" Peter answered, "Thou art the Christ, the Son of the living God." Jesus responded, "Blessed art thou...for flesh and blood hath not revealed it unto thee, but my Father which is in heaven" (Matt. 16:15-17).

Peter received that revelation from God, not from a priest or pastor. Likewise, as tears poured down my cheeks, I realized God had revealed this truth directly to me. It was as if He was saying, "Carolyn, flesh and blood has not revealed this to you, but my Father which is in heaven." If we would dare to listen, God would speak to each of us.

Trusting Him

Every day involves trusting our loving Father with who we are. He is all-powerful and all-knowing, and He wants us to be free from any lies we believe. I love the image "childlike trust," maybe because I've seen it in my own children. They ask God for anything—and know He always hears them.

When Randy was two years old, he played in the backyard where our dogs romped. At the dinner table one day we asked Randy to pray before we ate our meal. While our heads were bowed, he said sincerely, "Dear God, thank You for the food. And please help me get the poo poo off my cement truck." John and I coughed to choke our chuckles. Actually, Randy had exercised his childlike trust, telling God about a serious problem in his young life.

Another of our children displayed this kind of trust once when we all traveled by airplane to reach our vacation spot. Airplanes are my least favorite method of transportation. I pray before we take off; I pray during the flight; I pray while we land.

On this particular flight, we experienced what the pilot called "moderate chop." When we heard his announcement, John and I renamed it "chop suey" because of the queasy feeling in our stomachs. In the midst of our bumpy ride, Julianne leaned over to me and whispered, "Just think, Mommy, if something happens to this airplane, we'll already be halfway to heaven."

As I clutched the seat with both hands, I thought, *That's childlike trust.*

After the four-year-old son of a friend of mine skinned his knee, he learned what it means to trust in God. He ran to his mother crying, but not because of the cut. Anticipating his bathtime, he was afraid the water in the tub would make the cut sting. Matthew's mother suggested they pray for Jesus to heal the cut so it wouldn't sting. That evening she ran the bathwater. When he climbed into the tub, she was out of the bathroom for one reason or another and she heard her son scream. The mother raced to the bathroom and threw open the door.

"What is it, Matthew?" she blurted out anxiously.

His leg was under water, and he pointed to his knee. "Mother!" he exclaimed. "It doesn't sting. Let's give Jesus a clap offering!"

Recently I was reminded by my teenage son that simply trusting God in everything is His plan for us. Randy came walking in with a split lip he had gotten when romping with a dog in our neighborhood. The dog's claw had caught Randy's lip, leaving an ugly gash. Without thinking I immediately went into my typical mother reaction—yelling frantic instructions, running for ice, water, antiseptic, cloth. Randy stopped, looked at me with disgust and said, "Mother, I thought you'd pray for me instead of acting like this." Nothing catches me up short quicker than the truth from my own children—"out of the mouths of babes...."

A contemporary Christian song that was popular a few years ago expressed musically Jesus' teaching about childlike faith. "They don't know that I go running home when I fall down. They don't know Who picks me up when no one is around. I dry my eyes and look up to the Father for His smile. For deep inside the armor, the warrior is a child."[3]

In Ephesians 6, Paul lists the armor of God—the belt of truth, the breastplate of righteousness, the shoes of the gospel of peace, the shield of faith, the helmet of salvation and the sword of the Spirit. But underneath the armor, the warrior is a child. It all goes back to Hebrews 11:34, out of weakness we are made strong. In our weakness, we come to God in childlike trust and His strength becomes ours. His strength allows us to see who we are so we can become who He wants us to be: people who are transparent because Jesus' light shines through us.

THREE

Lord, Show Me

God's love for us is absolute and unconditional. It's total, and He asks that we love each other as He loves us (see John 13:34). Jesus also said that we are to love others as we love ourselves (see Matt. 22:39).

It's hard to love someone you don't know. And I'm not just talking about your spouse or neighbor. I'm talking about yourself.

If you don't know who you are, how can you have a healthy love and respect for yourself? And if you don't have a healthy love and respect for yourself, how can you love others or be honest and vulnerable with them?

John graduated from law school at Stetson University in 1968 and immediately went to work as a law clerk for a federal judge. Shortly thereafter, he was drafted and served in the navy's

Judge Advocate General Corps. We were eventually transferred to Corpus Christi, Texas, where we began to find out what it meant to live without masks.

A couple in our Sunday school class invited us over for dinner. John and I noticed something different about them. They could look at each other across the room and communicate without saying a word. But Gene and Ellen weren't just relating well; they were open and honest with each other, with us and with God. "What is it about you that makes you so open?" we asked.

This couple didn't mind talking about their relationship with God, nor did they mind talking about their relationship with each other. They could express their feelings for God and each other in a way that was foreign to us.

As far as I could tell, John was more concerned with personal ambition than with our having a happy marriage. We simply didn't communicate and therefore had a shallow relationship. We knew Gene and Ellen had something in their lives and marriage that we lacked, and we wanted it.

The two of them insisted that we attend a weekend couples' retreat at Laity Lodge in Leaky, Texas. Late in 1969 the four of us packed up and went. For two days we listened to other couples give their testimonies. For the first time in our lives, John and I were exposed to people who had a natural relationship with the living God. We transferred all of the head knowledge we had learned through our denominational upbringings into our hearts. We realized who God was, what

He wanted to do for us and how much He loved us. We also began to see that we did not know who we were. No wonder we didn't know each other. No wonder we lived behind masks.

Just As I Am?

"If you could be anyone in the world, who would you want to be?" a father asked his three sons while driving along in the car.

The oldest boy named a well-known sports figure. The second son chose somebody he admired. The youngest boy, a four-year-old, sat silently in the back seat. After driving a little farther, the father insisted Jimmy answer his question.

"Well, Dad," Jimmy muttered, "I just want to be me."

That's the answer the father wanted to hear. He had tried to develop in his sons a healthy self-esteem, always encouraging them to want to be themselves.

Soon after I heard that story, I decided to ask my daughter the same question. I was driving Julianne (we sometimes call her Julie) and her best friend home from kindergarten. First I asked her friend, "Jenny, if you could be anybody in the whole world, who would you be?"

"I would be Jesus," she answered immediately.

How beautiful, I sighed. Of course I expected my daughter to agree quickly, so I asked somewhat confidently, "Julie, who would you be?"

To my surprise, she quipped, "I'd be Wonder Woman." I wondered what I had done to instill such a dream.

Her answer may sound humorous, but it tells us something about ourselves.

How many of us know who we really are? How many of us accept ourselves as we are? How many of us are two different people—one who wears a mask to cover the one we're afraid to let anyone see?

Julianne is now 14, and I recently asked her what her response would be now. I was relieved to hear those self-accepting words, "I'm just happy being myself, Mom."

There's no one with whom I'd want to change places, but it's taken me years to get to this place. And this happened only as God showed me that He wants me to know who I am and to acknowledge my weaknesses so that He can make me transparent—and whole.

When we become Christians, "Old things are passed away; behold, all things are become new" (2 Cor. 5:17). When we accept Jesus, our old natures are passed away and we are new creatures in Christ. But that doesn't mean we aren't a product of everything that has happened to us from the time we were conceived.

Even though we receive salvation, we still maintain our personalities and characters. And that's what God wants to develop to the fullest. And the process starts when we're willing for it to start.

Being Willing

John's grandmother lived in a tiny town in Georgia. It was always a treat to talk to "Ma-Ma" on the telephone. As soon as she would pick up the phone she would start talking a mile a minute.

John used to make me so nervous when he'd be listening to her.

Because he loved her and didn't want to hurt her feelings by cutting her off, John would lay the receiver down, walk off, fix himself a snack or grab the newspaper. I warned him that she might take a breath any minute and discover that he wasn't listening. But he's always assured me, "Carolyn, there's no problem."

He was always right. Without fail, she would be talking away when he came back to the telephone.

One of her long stories points out the first step to transparency. The neighbors had been fighting. She explained, "John, it was just terrible. David rode up and then Sandra came out and yelled. He got in the car and sped off and she ran after him. The children were crying...."

His grandmother went on and on about it for ten minutes or more. Finally, she paused and added, "And I just couldn't look. I just couldn't look."

John couldn't resist. With a teasing tone he asked, "Well, Ma-Ma, if you couldn't look, how do you know all that happened?"

Without a moment's hesitation she answered, "I called Ethel next door, and she looked!"

Courage to Look

The first step to knowing who you are and becoming transparent is having the courage to look. I'm not talking about the courage to look at your neighbor. I'm talking about the courage it takes to look inside yourself at who you are.

Most people never do this. They never say, "Lord, You know who I am. Show me who I am. I am willing to look inside." You see, being vulnerable and transparent opens the door for Jesus to bring wholeness in our lives. When I am transparent, I'm not hiding anything—from God, from myself or from others. When I can be vulnerable and open, the walls and masks do not block light or truth. When we ask God to shine His light into those wounded places, when we ask Him to search our hearts and thoughts, He does! As we see the truth, it sets us free!

Psalm 139:23 and 24 are my favorite verses concerning the courage to look: "Search me, O God, and know my heart: try me, and know my thoughts: and see if there be any wicked way in me, and lead me in the way everlasting."

This scripture has been my prayer for years. Every time I get earnest about this verse, God starts to reveal new areas about me that need to be healed and made whole, shining His light on new places I've never even seen before. Sometimes I think, *Haven't I seen it all yet?* But as long as I'm on this journey to wholeness and transparency in Jesus, I know He always wants to reveal to me more about myself.

Two Different Faces

When you find the courage to look at yourself, the next step to transparency is seeing the difference between the person you are and the masked person you allow others to see.

Is there a difference? Is there a fragmented individual hiding behind a superficial religious facade? Are there wounded places of rejection, insecurity or fear masked with a smile and an "I'm fine." Are we bleeding and hurt but afraid that an admission of truth will make us less than spiritual? Less than an overcomer? It takes seeing the difference between what you are inside and what you project to the world that gives you the freedom to choose between the two.

Experiencing an honest, open walk with a vibrant personal relationship with God is the route to becoming whole.

It's because of Jesus' love for us that He wants us to have this freedom of being a whole person who knows himself and the God who made him.

If we are saying the right words but not being the right person, we aren't being transparent. I'm not saying that we shouldn't put our best foot forward. We all want to appear nice and wonderful. But we need to live out our lives without wearing masks, and we need to walk toward transparency as we walk toward wholeness.

Several years ago, a couple from our church dedicated their baby to the Lord during a Sunday morning service. The dedication ceremony was so beautiful—I cried all the way through it. As the mother cradled the infant in her arms, the parents sang a song for the special occasion. The baby smiled and cooed.

In the beauty of that moment, I remembered how different it had been for me on the day our daughter, Julianne, was dedicated. I was all prepared. The night before I had the baby's dress and bonnet all laid out. John and I got to church early; that in itself was a miracle. Our family sat together in the pew, and the minister announced, "Now will those parents dedicating their babies please come forward."

I held Julie in my arms and when I stood up, she threw up all over me, all over my dress, all over her gown, all over the diaper bag. I couldn't believe it, but I just kept walking to the front of the church. Our dear baby daughter then cried throughout the entire solemn ceremony.

Later when I watched the young couple dedicate their baby during a perfect ceremony, I thought, *Why couldn't this have happened with Julie's dedication?*

If you will be honest with me, if you have ever had a baby dedicated, what's the one thing you worry about? *My baby is going to cry in front of the whole congregation.* Right? You see, we all want to put our best foot forward. There's nothing wrong with that.

But we must see the difference between what we are projecting and who we really are in Christ: Jesus was never pretentious. He was Himself. He never put on airs or assumed an aura of superiority. He was Himself. He wants the same for us. Each of us is a unique person with strengths and weaknesses, but when we hide the weaknesses, the walls go up. You only see my strengths; you put up walls to match my perfection, and the damaging separation begins.

Like a friend of mine says, "Instead of *singing* 'Just as I am,' it's *being* 'Just as I am.' "

Lord, Here I Am

When you identify the differences between who you are and whom you allow others to see, then the next step to transparency is admitting the discrepancy to yourself and God. Cecil Osborne writes,

> Tell God how you feel. If you feel hostility, tell Him so. He knows all about human hostility in general and yours in particular. Don't justify it or rationalize it—confess it.

> Tell Him about your jealousy or envy, your greed, your lust for people and things. Confess your fear and lack of faith and self-righteousness, the critical attitudes which cause you to judge others and justify yourself. Confess the self-sufficiency which has caused you to depend upon yourself more than upon God.

> Tell Him about your self-pity which you used as a device to get sympathy. Tell Him the whole sordid story of your deceit. Go back and dredge up the past, the petty gossip, and the emotional insecurity which prompted it. Tell Him the lies you've told, or the silent deceit you engaged in when no lie was told. Above all tell Him how unforgiving and unloving you have been.[1]

None of us likes to admit that we feel any of these things. But in truth, because we are human, we've all had to deal with them at one point or another. Some, more than others.

Feelings Aren't Right or Wrong

You may have never heard this before, but I

hope you will underline it. Feelings are not right or wrong; it's what you do with them that counts. You can suppress them or even deny them, but what you feel you feel.

So much emphasis has been placed on the fact that we walk by faith and not by sight. It is important to walk in faith even when we don't feel like it. But we often negate the fact that we are also emotional beings. God made us that way. How many times have you heard someone say, "You shouldn't feel that way"? And then we feel guilty on top of the way we already feel because we *do* feel "that way."

Jesus experienced every emotion common to humans. There isn't any emotion you feel that He doesn't already know and understand. It's important to look at your emotions and admit your feelings. They're already there. It's what you do with those feelings that is important. How can we deal with those emotions if we won't admit them even to ourselves. I have seen so many "up tight" people who wear a pious mask claiming the victory and are pent up with rage, insecurity or numerous feelings they refuse to admit. Jesus wants to show us what is there so He can do something about it.

A person can go to a psychiatrist and learn how to look inside and find out who he is. A woman may get it all out on the table and understand, for example, how her insecurities as a child have influenced her adult life. But then the psychiatrist can't make the individual change. A psychiatrist can't bring freedom.

But Jesus can. We can look at who we are, but

without the Healer we can't be made whole. On the other hand, we may know the Healer, but never let Him help us look inside ourselves. One without the other won't work.

We must trust God enough to know that He will accept us even if we admit what is going on inside of us.

Revealing and Healing

One of God's principles is that He reveals and then He heals. Let's take the example of a shy person who is afraid of crowds. That person prays, "God, please take away this fear." But God wants to show that person why he is insecure about being around a lot of people. Then He can heal the insecurity. Or take the man who was rejected as a child and told he would never measure up. As an adult, he proves himself to be highly successful financially, constantly trying to prove himself worthy to parents long since deceased. God wants to reveal to him that wounded rejected place so He can heal it.

I've had lots of hurting places in my own life, and I didn't even know what they were until God wanted to enter the basement of my life. He said, "Carolyn, you've let Me into the living room and the dining room and that's fine. But there's an area down in the basement underneath the stairs where you have never looked. That's what I want to focus on, and that's what I want to heal." Most of us make sure the entrance to our homes is presentable for guests. But are we as willing to open the closets? What about the attic—those hidden rooms where dust collects and where we don't go very often? If Jesus was a guest in your home, would you let Him look there?

It's not easy. It hurts. But it certainly is worth it.

As I've said, when I wear my mask and you wear yours, we are separated. That's the way Satan likes it. But a mask or a barrier does more than shut out another person. When you live behind a mask or a barrier to hide wounds such as anger, resentment, insecurity, pride, fear, guilt or anxiety, you block out all light. Soon you feel separated from God.

God showed me that a barrier is like masking a wound that gets infected. One time my son had impetigo. I found a little scab on his face, but I passed it off as "no problem," thinking the scab was a sure sign of healing. When I found another little scab on his finger and still another on his hand, I took him to the doctor who said, "I want you to go home and take the scabs off. Then I want you to clean and clean and clean those sores."

God emphasized to me that it's the same way with the wounds in my life. If I don't take off the mask or scab and clean out the sore, it soon spreads to another area. Wounds or sores such as bitterness and anger have an insidious way of spreading—popping up here and there.

Now cleaning it out means you have to look at it. Have you ever seen anybody clean a wound without looking at it? Even though it hurts, looking at and cleaning it are necessary so the wound won't spread. Masking the wound only hides the infection.

God Wants Our Best

Walking with Jesus in a personal relationship demands open communication, no barriers, no masks. If there is a barrier between us and God, it's never He. It's always us. He is always reaching out to us, always trying to get our attention, always trying to minister to us.

Consider the familiar picture of Jesus standing outside a door and knocking on it. Have you ever noticed that the artist painted no handle on the outside of the door? The door can be opened from the inside only.

It's our decision. Are we going to open the door, let Him in and let Him heal those places that hurt—or are we going to keep the door shut? God won't push the door open for us.

Cecil Osborne points out,

> In the Sermon on the Mount, Jesus taught spiritual, philosophical, psychological, and sociological principles; he discussed lawsuits, prayer, divorce, anxiety, love, forgiveness, reconciliation, anger, and a score of other things which pertained to everyday living. Jesus was interested in everything which concerned men, and His loving concern tells us that this is the nature of God—that He is interested in every detail of our lives."[2]

He wants to be involved in everything; every part of our lives is so significant that God is aware and present.

Not long ago John was driving along the interstate near our home. He doesn't pay much attention to the speedometer, and Julianne kept warning him, "Daddy, you're going too fast. You'd better slow down." He didn't pay much attention to her, either. A few miles later, she said, "Daddy, there's a policeman behind us." And he didn't pay a whole lot of attention to that until the red light started flashing. "Daddy, the light's going around," Julie reported.

John pulled over and rolled down his window. The policeman walked up to the car, and, before either man said anything, Julie blurted out, "I am so glad you are here. I have been praying someone would come along and tell my dad not to speed."

The police officer saw the look on John's face and just turned around and walked away. John's a little more careful about watching the speed limit now, but that story just shows how God does work all things together for good—even with a sense of humor.

In every difficult situation, each of us has a choice to make. We can either praise God and draw nearer to Him or block God out of our problems. We can say either, "God, help me," or, "When I get all this straightened out, Lord, then You and I will walk together again."

Sometimes we put our problem in the wrong perspective—placing it between God and us. The problem becomes so big that we can't see God. Or we blame Him, thinking, *Lord, You did this to me.*

But we have another alternative. We can put the problem behind us and draw close to God, saying, "Lord, You and I can handle anything. The two of us will work this problem out together."

My cousin Shirley phoned me one day. She's been going through a terrible time, and I advised her to reach out to God. "Let Him love you," I said. "Let your friends who know Him minister to you."

She was silent for a minute and then replied, "I've been doing just the opposite. I've withdrawn and pulled away from God and others and I didn't even know I was doing it."

"That's Satan's favorite trick," I continued. "If he can isolate you, then you won't get any help." Shirley realized she'd put her problem between her and God. Instead, she could have drawn closer to God and put the problem behind her. She had let it become a barrier against everyone who was concerned about her.

After we have admitted those places where we block His light, the next step is daring to be vulnerable with others as well as with God.

Transparency Comes
When We're Vulnerable

When we are vulnerable, real communication and relationship begin but sometimes being vulnerable hurts.

When I first let Jesus shine His light through me, I opened up to a cousin some of those places where I was growing. I remember explicitly her remark when I finished sharing that less than perfect side of me that I had carefully hidden for so long.

"Oh," she said, "that's too bad. We don't have any problems." I still recall that sinking feeling in my stomach. My first inclination was to gather up the emotional debris and shove it under the rug. I could have covered it up again successfully but at that point in my life, I made a conscious decision to go forward as a transparent person. I knew that was the only way toward wholeness. And I also knew that behind my cousin's mask lay wounds that needed healing. Perhaps at some point, when she was ready or willing to look inside, she'd remember I had refused to hold up a mask and would let me see behind the facade.

Transparency can bring freedom. If you know my foot slips, then you can admit yours does too. This freedom is often symbolized by our ability to laugh at ourselves.

Last winter our family went skiing in Colorado. The weather was perfect, and all five of us were "never-evers" in ski school. We had the suits, the poles, the skis and all kinds of other paraphernalia. And *some* of us had ability. I quickly found out that being poised on the slopes is fine if you're standing still, but when moving, survival means being knock-kneed and pigeon-toed with your rear sticking out—at least that's how it was for me. I'd always thought a *wedge* was a sandwich. But I found out it was my key to fighting panic as I raced out of control down the mountain. By the third day, I had fallen hundreds of times.

Every day the ski instructors would tactfully say, "Carolyn, perhaps you'd be more comfortable with this new group that's forming," instead of "Honey, you're so bad—we're moving you back." I did get the prize for meeting the most people, however, because I got a new beginner's group each day. I'm not exaggerating when I say I was absolutely terrible. Had I known I'd be as bad in advance, I wouldn't have bought a hot pink ski suit never to be forgotten by 300 Vail instructors. John called me the "Queen of the Virgin Wedge." But the same John that gave me that title also knows how to be transparent. His account of hobbling off the chair lift with one ski and struggling to keep his ski bib from falling in the toilet kept us in stitches. We're all human. If I let you see my frailty, you can drop your guard as well. When we are honest, we allow others that same freedom.

God wants to help us have the courage to look at ourselves, see the difference between who we are and what we project ourselves to be, admit that difference to ourselves and God, and dare to be vulnerable in open, honest relationships. This opens the door toward wholeness. Let's examine some of the specific barriers in our lives that God wants to reveal and heal to bring that wholeness. It is then that we know who we really are and who God wants us to be.

Assignment for Living

1. Read Psalm 139.
2. Make Psalm 139:23,24 your prayer. Write the verses on a piece of paper and tape the paper to your refrigerator door or a mirror, wherever you'll see it most often: "Search me, O God, and know my heart: try me, and know my thoughts: and see if there be any wicked way in me, and lead me in the way everlasting."
3. Ask yourself these questions:
    a. What mask do I wear?
    b. Could I be real before someone else so that he can do the same?
4. Talk to God about these questions:
    a. Lord, what is there in my life I don't understand?
    b. Lord, what is it about me that I have never given You to make whole?

You need to press on and do what God leads you to do in dealing with your emotions. I understand this will be difficult. Psalm 139 will help in dealing with these areas.

5. Pray this prayer: Dear God, I praise You because You know me inside and out. Nothing about me is hidden from You. Lord, I pray that You will give me the courage to look at myself. And, Lord, even if I've never looked inside, help me trust You and love You enough to let You look inside. I know You're knocking and I pray that You will help me open the door and let You into the attic or basement of my life, into the part I've never wanted You to see because I don't want to see it myself. Amen.

PART II

LOOKING PAST THE BARRIERS:

Show Me The Wounds

FOUR

Dealing With Anger And Resentment

Before we were married John took me to his hometown in southwest Georgia to introduce me to his family. I met all the aunts and uncles, the grandmothers, everyone. Of course I was nervous because I wanted to make a good impression by doing the right things.

We'd had a wonderful time and were getting ready to leave when one of John's uncles took me aside. He said, "Carolyn, I just want to tell you that there has never been a cross word in our family."

My first thought was, *Oh no, what a tradition to live up to!* It turned out that John had overheard his uncle's statement to me. When we were driving away, John grinned and said, "Carolyn, let me explain something to you. Do you know why there has never been a cross word in my family?"

"No," I replied, almost afraid to hear the answer.

"It's because most of them don't speak to each other," he quipped.

Now *there* was one thick barrier.

Even though it's not acknowledged, anger and resentment separate us from each other and from God. My own family hasn't been exempt from the devastation these wounds can cause. When my dad was sixteen years old, my grandparents left their church following a disagreement with the preacher over playing cards. Now wasn't that important! The family never darkened the doors of a church again. Their children grew up unchurched, and to this day none of those children even speaks to each other.

You see, little resentments can magnify themselves until they are so big that communication stops. These high, thick walls are almost impossible to penetrate, except by the light of God's love.

Me? Angry?

In polite company, anger always has had a bad name—especially among us Southerners, known for our charm, and especially among us Christians, who constantly read and hear that we are to be patient and loving and forgiving. We read 1 Corinthians 13, the chapter that details the qualities of love, and we panic that we are so far from who we think we should be.

Lots of times we say, "Well, I've just turned my emotions or the problem that caused them over to God." But we really haven't turned them over at all. We're still carrying around all the resentment or anger. Instead of allowing God to work in us, to heal those wounds of anger and resentment that keep us from being all we could be, we "boot strap" or "bottle cap" our anger. What do I mean by that?

Those are my phrases for the way we deny that our anger or resentment exists. We convince ourselves that we don't feel this way. "I do not have anger," we say. "There is nothing wrong with me. I feel charitable toward God, my neighbor and myself." But how hard we work to believe our own lies.

I have a friend who had one of the most beautiful walks with the Lord I've ever seen. She taught me much in my own spiritual journey, and I marveled at how clearly she heard from God. But tragedy struck her life, and she blamed God and repressed her anger, shoving it down deep. As that boot-strapped anger gradually boiled to the surface, she refused to go to church or read the Word or heed the counsel of Christians urging her back. And today she is separated from that close walk with a loving heavenly Father because resentment toward God has permeated her life.

What a price we pay when we choose to walk away from God. Isaiah 50:10,11 says: "Who among you fears the Lord and obeys his Servant? If such men walk in darkness, without one ray of light, let them trust the Lord, let them rely upon their God. But see here, you who live in your *own* light, and warm yourselves from your own fires and not from God's; you will live among sorrows" (TLB). When we choose our own light and not

God's we choose a life of sorrow. By not taking a step toward God's light, we automatically step away. There's no limbo. Our heart keeps beating, our lungs keep breathing, time keeps ticking and all the while God reaches out in tender mercy entreating us to choose His way.

Perhaps you have resentments that have crept in. They start small—picky attitudes God wants to set straight—but they turn into big problems if they aren't dealt with. Is there boot-strapped anger underneath the surface? Or is it bottle-capped waiting for something to set it off? When we bottle cap our anger, we keep going along with all this negative emotion inside us. Soon some insignificant event makes the cap fly off and out pours the fizz. Of this I am certain: One way or another our anger eventually comes out.

I have a friend who bottle caps her anger. To her, submission to her husband is parallel to being a doormat. She keeps her thoughts and feelings hidden and never expresses to him what she thinks or how she feels. These bottle-capped emotions are held in check most of the time, but sometimes in the presence of friends she will blow up over nothing. The bottle-capped anger is going to come out somewhere—even though misguided and misdirected. To her it's not proper to tell her husband how she feels, but her friends often see the explosion because she hasn't resolved the anger inside her.

A Better Way

There are three steps we need to take to release anger—or any other emotion, such as fear, insecurity, anxiety or pride. The first is to *discover* the emotion.

We are all made up of three parts—the physical, the mental and the spiritual.

We place much emphasis on our physical bodies. The importance of good nutrition, keeping physically fit and the general emphasis on health and longevity takes up much of our attention. There is an abundance of spas, fitness clubs, weight loss centers, not to mention the emphasis on fashion, color coordination and make-up.

Our mental capacities are being expanded constantly. The emphasis on education, good grades, better jobs, a computerized society requiring more skills is a constant challenge to spend more energy on the mental part of our make-up.

But our spiritual beings often stay in diapers, in part because we never open up inside; it hurts too much.

We can focus on the outer aspects of worshipping and praising God and never look inside at what He wants to change in us. I know many people who come to church week after week. They lift their hands to the Lord. They sincerely praise Him, but they're living crummy, rotten lives because they won't look inside themselves at what He wants to change.

I counseled with a wife who couldn't see her anger and resentment toward her alcoholic husband. During our conversation, I offered alternatives, things she could do to strengthen her marriage. She responded by saying, "I'm not angry and I'm not bitter. I'm just waiting for the day I can bury him and get on with my life." Sadly, her own words revealed the anger she refused to acknowledge.

Resentments have a way of growing into anger. When they start, resentments may be caused by any number of things—insecurity, jealousy, simple friction between different types of personalities. But no matter what their origin, they can start small and then Satan can build on them until they're out of hand. I clearly recall one instance where I had to discover a resentment before I could, with God's help, break down the barrier that was building and isolating me from God and my neighbor.

I had to be around a certain woman every day for a whole year. Unconsciously I backed away from her because she was very harsh and loud. When we were grouped together with other women, I'd talk to someone else, trying to avoid her. Even though I was aware of how I disliked the woman's personality, I didn't realize I was withdrawing from her until the Holy Spirit nudged me.

While driving one day, I was praying and the Holy Spirit brought her face before me in my mind's eye. I sensed the Spirit speaking these words to me, "Carolyn, I have been noticing how you've been acting toward this person—your lack of attention to her."

Right then and there I had to choose whether or not I would walk toward wholeness or turn my back on it. With God's help I had discovered my negative feeling. It was up to me to take the second step—to *admit* my resentment, which could have grown to anger, to myself and to God.

In my heart, I acknowledged what the Lord was revealing to me about myself. He reminded me that she was one of His children and that He loved her. "Yes, Lord," I admitted, "I see that. I'm sorry, I confess my petty resentment to You and ask Your forgiveness. I'll make an honest effort to love her."

That opened the door for the next thing I needed to do to deal with my negative emotion.

After that discovery, I prayed for her occasionally. As time went by, I reached out to her whether I wanted to or not. I made an effort to be nice to her every day. You see, Jesus is the "feeling changer." As I acknowledged the resentment and laid it at His feet, He changed those negative feelings in me. I reached out in love as an act of my will, and He filled me with compassion for this person I had avoided so carefully.

She had a hard time sharing with anyone on a personal level because she'd built big, thick barriers around herself. One particular day, she opened up a little and described a financial problem in her family. "I don't know what I'm going to do about it," she said. "It's just breaking our hearts."

I was thunderstruck by her being so open with me; I gave her a routine reply. Without even thinking, I said, "I'm sorry. I'll pray for you." And I really meant it, but I knew my words sounded hollow.

Later, God told me why my words sounded

hollow: "There are no hands and feet to those prayers. I want you to meet her need."

I was absolutely overwhelmed that God would take my crummy, rotten, resentful attitude and turn it around for His glory by giving me a chance to do something for Him.

John and I supplied the woman's financial need on an anonymous basis. Afterward, we found out she was not a Christian and she received the monetary gift as from the Lord. It showed her how much God loved her.

God, I Need Help

Often our resentment or anger stems from wrongs done to us by others. We have a hard time defining our anger as the wound it is because we feel our negative feelings are justified by our pain. "Why should I forgive?" we ask—especially when we've never received an apology.

Once I got a letter from another friend who had been treated very badly most of her life. Her husband had ignored, belittled and criticized her. Now he wanted out of the marriage just as they were getting on their feet financially. She had worked to put him through school, and now it appeared he didn't need her anymore.

"People are telling me I have to forgive," she wrote. "I don't understand why I have to forgive my husband. Look at what he has done to me."

She had good reasons for resentment. She had been wronged, and it hurt. And he *was* acting like a jerk! But God speaks very explicitly about forgiveness. (I didn't write the Book!) He didn't say, "Forgive only if it's justified. Forgive when you get around to it. Forgive if you feel like it. Please forgive." He flatly said, "If you don't forgive others, I won't forgive you" (see Matt. 6:15). And why do you think He put that in there? It was for our own good. Unforgiveness is a killer. It eats us up inside and we are the ones who lose.

I know forgiveness isn't easy. I recently received a letter from a relative who attacked my husband. I was so angry I had to run around our golf course for three days praying in the Spirit and forgiving that person as an act of my will. Finally, Jesus, in His healing mercy, took those angry feelings away. But He couldn't have done that had I not been *willing* to let them go. It is hard, especially when the anger seems justified.

Forgiveness is a decision, an act of the will. It's something we choose to do. We must choose to say, "Lord, I understand that this unforgiveness is not what You want me to hold inside. I'll tell You everything about this situation that makes me unforgiving. I'll tell You the whole thing. And, Lord, I make the decision to give it up."

Tell God everything you're feeling and ask Him to show you the reason for your feelings. Why does it hurt so much? Then you're ready to go through the process of giving up the anger and the pain.

God's command that we must forgive may sound extreme, but He does not leave us to gut out forgiveness totally on our own. When we show Him our willingness, He can and does change our emotions.

Years ago, I counseled with a woman who had

gone through a terrible divorce and felt extreme rejection. We had reached the point of her needing to rid herself of anger through forgiveness and she said, "I can't do it. I can't forgive him for what he did."

"All right, I understand," I said. "The pain is so great. Let's back up another step. Let's ask God to make you willing to forgive your ex-husband." So we prayed together.

After about a month, she reached the point of saying, "Now I can do it. I'm willing to forgive him." We may discover our anger and admit it, but the healing process isn't complete until we are willing to give it up and no longer feel entitled to it—no matter what its origin.

Day in and Day Out

I wish I could say we forgive one time and it's over; forget it, the end. But sometimes it isn't that easy. I believe that's why Jesus referred to forgiving more than once, knowing that we would like to draw the line on how much is enough before our anger is justified and vindicated. Peter was hoping for that justification when he asked Jesus if seven times was enough.

"Jesus saith unto him, 'I say not unto thee, until seven times: but, until seventy times seven' " (Matt. 18:22). Sometimes we get kicked and we forgive, and we get kicked again and we forgive again. It isn't easy. When those feelings come back, realize that you may not be able to get rid of them, but Jesus can. He's the feeling-changer.

Not long ago, we went through a very painful experience. Some dear friends of ours had been wronged and I had wholeheartedly taken on their hurt. I knew I had to forgive all the people involved. It was difficult but I did. Then later, all those emotions would come back again and I'd find myself full of resentment. *No,* I would say to myself, *I made the decision to forgive. I refuse to hold on to unforgiveness. God, as an act of my will, I forgive them.*

Forgiveness is a daily process. Why? Because new irritations constantly pop into our lives.

I've heard Jack Hayford give an excellent example of this. He boarded an airplane and immediately became annoyed with the stewardess for hanging his garment bag in the wrong compartment. While walking down the narrow aisle of the plane, he brushed against a little boy who was already seated. A color marker in the boy's hand left a bright stripe on Jack's pant leg. He sat in his seat put out with everybody. But God confronted him about his angry feelings. He had to say, "God, I'm sorry. I forgive the stewardess. I forgive the little boy." Jack Hayford had to deal with his anger and resentment and the blame he placed on others for making his life temporarily miserable.

A Story of Forgiveness

Forgiveness is just one step to wholeness in Jesus. When I received the baptism in the Holy Spirit, God showed me that Jesus is the answer to physical healing, emotional healing and deliverance. No matter how hard we try, He isn't going to be put in a box. He will use whatever avenue He chooses to make us whole.

I want to share with you an example of the

impact of forgiveness in my life. I shudder to think what might have happened had I not forgiven.

Years ago when John and I lived in Texas, we were members of a witnessing team at Laity Lodge—the retreat center where we experienced the heart knowledge of God's great love for us. On this particular weekend, six of us, three couples, were to give our testimonies.

Before we left for the lodge, I had it all figured out for the Lord. I would be the first to speak about the things God had taught me. I would get my testimony over with so I could enjoy the rest of the weekend.

When we arrived, the man in charge of the retreat center asked another member of our team to give his testimony Friday night. "Then we'll wait and see what happens tomorrow," he said.

I thought, *That's all right. I won't speak Friday night. I'll be the first one Saturday morning and still have the rest of the weekend to relax.*

Saturday morning came. I wasn't first, second or third. In fact, I didn't speak on Saturday at all, and by evening I was a little unnerved. God obviously had other plans for me, but I wanted to know what they were.

I finally asked Him, "Lord, do you want me to say what I'd planned to say?" His answer was a definite no.

Later, the head of the retreat center came up to me and said, "Carolyn, you're going to be last. I want you to give these people a good send-off. Give them something to feel really good about." Little did he know that that wasn't

God's plan either.

When it was my turn to speak, I got up in front of all those people and cried for two hours. I told them I couldn't say the things I'd planned to say. Rather I shared how God had spoken to me during the weekend about forgiving my dad for the things he had done while I was growing up. I had to forgive my dad for breaking up our home and family and for his problem with alcohol. I had to forgive him for not loving me the way I had wanted. But I wondered, if I were to forgive him, would that somehow negate all the pain my mother had experienced? Would I be turning my back on all her suffering?

In this difficult time God showed me that the pain I had suffered had been the by-product of a wounded, bleeding man hiding behind his own insecurities and fears. Because those wounds in his life had never been healed, they became the wedge that led to the drinking and the death of a marriage. Somehow seeing that the pain and rejection weren't directed at me seemed to make a difference. I saw a man, a product of his background, reacting out of his own set of problems, not willing *or knowing how* to grasp the only One who could heal those wounds. And I saw that in my own unforgiveness, I had not been a channel through which the unconditional love of a merciful God could flow.

As I released these deep painful feelings, I saw that my dad might not have realized the hurt he had caused me. But at that point only one thing mattered: my willingness to forgive him.

Sharing all that with those people was difficult for me, but afterward many came to me and said, "I didn't want to hear that, but it was exactly what I needed."

Shortly after that weekend in 1971, we moved from Corpus Christi to Orlando because the navy transferred John to another base. My dad was living near Orlando at that time. He and my mother had divorced seven years earlier, after twenty-five years of marriage. Following our move to Florida, I reached out to my dad as I'd never before been able. With the Lord's help, we established a close relationship again. One time, in particular, when he came to our house, I put my arms around him and said, "I love you."

At that point in my life, I felt a real burden to know he'd accepted Jesus Christ as his Savior. I knew his life-style certainly was not that of a Christian, and I prayed for an opportunity to talk to Dad about the Lord.

If you had known my dad then, you would know that this was like Esther approaching the king, hoping he would hold out the scepter of acceptance. Anytime I would bring up such a subject, it would get put down.

For four years, I prayed for his salvation. Finally, in 1975, God gave me the opportunity to talk to him. By that time, he was remarried, to Gerry, a woman like my mother in some ways.

They lived in Sarasota and, when our family went there to spend a week at the beach, I arranged to meet my dad for lunch. Twice he completely forgot our date, which was unlike him. Yet

I was determined that God would win. On the last day of our stay, we got together at a restaurant for lunch.

This man, who never expresses any emotion, sat there and cried while I talked about God. For the first time in his life he opened the doors and tore down the walls. He felt sure that God couldn't accept him. He told me things he'd never told anyone about his childhood and war experiences.

I assured my dad of God's love for him, and I asked the question that had been on my mind. "If you died today, Daddy, do you know where you'd go?" I let him know it was important to me that he spend eternity with Jesus.

After that day, I prayed that he would walk with God daily. His life changed very little; the drinking didn't stop. It's amazing, though, how God never takes His hand off someone. He still keeps trying to get a person's attention.

In 1979, Gerry telephoned us. "Carolyn," she said, "your father has had a heart attack. He is in intensive care. I can see him only once an hour for five minutes. No one else is allowed in, so you needn't rush down here. At this point, we just don't know anything."

I talked frequently to Gerry and the nurses, asking them to relay messages: "Tell my father to live." "Tell my dad I'm praying for him." "Tell my dad he's going to get better." The hours stretched into days, and we kept sending him these encouraging messages, even though he didn't respond to any of them.

Eventually, his condition improved and he was

moved out of intensive care into a room where he was still closely monitored. Every day I would call and leave him a message.

I knew he was getting better when I asked the nurse if he was ornery, and she said emphatically, "Oh, yes."

"Has he complained about the food yet?" I inquired.

"Yes, as a matter of fact he had the head chef up here this morning telling him everything that was wrong with the food." We laughed, and the nurse continued, "But he ordered two trays of food and ate both of them."

A few days later he phoned me and said, "Carolyn, I want to thank you for the calls, cards and letters. Your flowers make this place look like a funeral parlor, but I'm doing better. I wish they'd let me out of here. The food is terrible...." He went on and on and then he paused, adding, "There's only one problem."

"What's that, Daddy?" I quickly responded.

"Well, the doctors took two electrocardiograms that showed extensive heart damage. Then this morning they took another EKG...and it's all clear." He sounded puzzled.

Before I even thought about what I was saying, out of my mouth came the words, "God healed you, Daddy, to show you how much He loves you."

My father just fell apart at the other end of the line. When he regained his composure, he replied, "Well, I suppose that's possible."

I questioned him, "Daddy, how else would you

explain the difference in the EKGs?'' He cried again.

Not long after that I called my mother who had been the head of the EKG department in a Daytona hospital for ten years. I told her about the results of Dad's electrocardiograms. She said, "Carolyn, that's not possible. You don't get a clear EKG after you have had extensive heart damage. The damage will show up on every test taken from then on. There isn't any explanation except that his heart was totally miraculously healed.''

Now I submit to you that, had I not been willing to forgive my Dad fourteen years ago, through my unforgiveness Satan might have blocked my ability to share with him, bring him to the Lord and pray him through.

The Lord only knows where Dad would be today if I had not forgiven him. I don't get any gold stars for that. God didn't give us a choice. He commanded us to let go of our anger and resentment— to forgive. In forgiving as an act of my will I open the floodgates of healing in my life—the process by which the great ''feeling-changer'' heals those scars of unforgiveness so long held and nurtured. As I dared to look inside at the pain, to be vulnerable and open, the healing power of God began to bring wholeness into my life.

Assignment for Living

1. Read these scriptures as they relate to anger and resentment: Ephesians 4:31; 4:26; 6:4; Psalm 37:8; Proverbs 29:22; 14:29; 15:1; James 1:19.

2. Ask yourself these questions prayerfully, asking God to reveal His truth to you:

   a. Is there anger or resentment buried deep inside me? Do I boot strap or bottle cap my anger?

   b. Does it manifest itself in sickness (internalized) or an unaccountable fit of rage (externalized)?

   c. Am I harboring unforgiveness in any area of my life?

   d. Is anger keeping the fire of unforgiveness going?

   e. Am I resentful in certain situations toward certain people? Why?

   f. Have small resentments become larger because they weren't dealt with?

   g. Do I have unforgiveness toward God? For what do I blame Him?

3. These are difficult questions to ask and difficult to look at because they're not pretty. None of us likes to admit anger and resentments. But God already knows and is waiting to heal those sores. Have courage to confess how you feel. Tell Him every detail and lay it at His feet. He's able to help you discover and admit these areas of anger and frustration and to bind up the broken hurting places. Let His forgiveness flow through you as you

forgive others.

4. Pray: Dear Lord, Thank You for accepting me when I don't like what I see about myself. Thank You for assuring me in Your Word that absolutely nothing can separate me from Your love. Please, Lord, give me courage to look at anger and resentment in my life. I want to become whole and give up this pain. I choose to forgive. Help me through my struggle to admit these areas to You and heal my wounded heart. Thank You, Lord. Amen.

FIVE

Overcoming Insecurity and Rejection

Years ago, I knew a man who, as a child, had been repeatedly told that he was a failure; he'd never amount to anything. No matter what he accomplished in life, it was not good enough. He grew up to be terribly insecure. He got within two credit hours of graduating from college and then dropped out. Throughout his entire life, he would come to the brink of success and quit. As a child, failure was so ingrained in him that he couldn't break the pattern. As an adult, he lived up to that same image.

I had been sharing with his sister about the baptism in the Holy Spirit, about praying for healing and believing God. She was a friend of mine and was growing in the Lord. About this time, their mother entered the hospital for gall bladder surgery. On the day of the operation, I felt that I needed to be in that waiting room with the family. I didn't especially want to, and I couldn't figure out why I was supposed to, but I felt compelled to go.

In the weeks before the mother's hospitalization, we had prayed that God would heal her so the surgery would not be necessary. Even though the nurses were preparing the woman for the operation that day, I strongly urged the family to order one more set of X-rays before the surgery.

I believed God had healed her. "No, no, no," they argued. "It's all set. This is the way it's going to be." *OK, Lord,* I prayed silently, *I'm willing to do what You want me to do in this situation.* And I was about to find out whether or not I meant it.

The family and I, including the son with the failure complex, sat there in the waiting room as the mother went into surgery. Finally the surgeon came out and leaned against the doorpost. He pulled off his surgical cap and his face was pale.

"Well, I don't know what to say," he began. "We opened her up, and there were no gallstones. I can't explain it." The surgeon just shook his head and walked down the hall.

At that moment, I sensed the Holy Spirit asking me if I was ready to speak. My first reaction was, *Oh no, I don't want to say this. They are going to think I'm crazy.* I know that the Holy Spirit speaks to each of us differently. But when the Spirit speaks to me, I have a choice. Either I can do what He says or run around the building sixteen times out of frustration for not obeying.

66

Obediently, I raised my hand to get their attention and said, "I believe God healed your mother before surgery. I believe God wants you to understand how much He loves you and how He wants to be a part of your lives."

This son, who lived in failure, sat there and looked at me. "I can't accept that, Carolyn," he said, shaking his head. And two weeks later he took his own life.

I had no way of knowing that that man was going to commit suicide, but I believe God went up to the last minute of this son's life trying to get his attention. God was saying to him, "You are not a failure. Because of Me, you are worthy. Because of Me, you can do wonderful things. Reach out of yourself and trust Me." But the man would not listen.

God reached out in love to this troubled life, reminding me of a scripture that I love so much. Jesus stood on the hillside overlooking Jerusalem and cried, "O Jerusalem, Jerusalem...how often would I have gathered thy children together, even as a hen gathereth her chickens under her wings, and ye would not!" (Matt. 23:37). God wants to heal the insecurity that has kept us suffering for so long.

Parental Influence

Insecurity usually stems from a poor self-image. An insecure person does not feel good about who he or she is. Often, insecurity develops during childhood, as a result of a parent who says to a child, "You dummy. You idiot. You're stupid. You'll never amount to anything." The child looks at the parent as an authority figure comparable to God; the parent must be right.

That's when insecurity begins. The child starts the pattern of living up to what Mom and Dad have said. Mask wearing also begins because the child pretends to be someone other than who he really is. The child thinks, *I'm not so good. I have these faults. I'll act differently so nobody will see the real me.* This feeling that we don't measure up can have a profound effect on our lives.

Satan isn't fair. He dumps rejection on us when we are at our weakest, when we don't know any better. He doesn't wait until we know how to stand against him and fight him.

John and I have three adopted children. We laid hands on all three of them as infants and stood against rejection from the womb. A mother might have had feelings of rejection toward her child, thinking, *What am I going to do? Here is this baby I don't want.*

Cecil Osborne says,

The rejected child always feels guilty. Although a child does not think it out in these terms, the resultant feeling is "I am rejected and unloved. If I were a good child, they would love me. Since I'm not loved, I must be bad." The result is a deep feeling of guilt and unworthiness. The rejected child says, "I'm not loved, so it's my fault."[1]

If we don't overcome rejection, we grow up to be adults repeating a childhood pattern. Sometimes a pattern isn't obvious, and the discovery of the underlying issue is critical to one's healing. A boy who was brought up in an unloving environment may grow up to be a very stingy man. His frugality may simply be financial insecurity— or a transferred emotional insecurity.

Peer Pressure

Insecurity also happens as a result of peer pressure.

When I was nine years old, we moved from California to Florida. It was an emotional time for me. For the first couple of years after the move, I was bounced back and forth by the leaders of the cliques. You know how little girls can be about "She's my friend, and you're not." Well, best friends changed at the whim of the group leaders, and the rejection hurt terribly. I wanted to be accepted socially so badly that I worked to prove I could be all things to all people. For example, I eventually became president of every club I joined. I had to set the grade curve in every class. Straight A's were all I would accept.

By the time I was in junior high, I had to be everybody's best friend. I had the titles, the honors. Eventually, I had all those things that made people say, "Isn't she something?" But inside I was a mess. All I could think about was, *Do they like me? What do they think of what I said? Are they talking about me?*

As an adult, I would leave a roomful of people and think, *I wonder what they thought about what I said?* Because of my insecurity of not being accepted by other people, I focused on *me, me, me.*

I didn't know why I had that problem until I started reading God's Word and praying. I said, "God, show me why I have so much anxiety about what other people think of me." That's when He started to shine His light on my life. He showed me that I was repeating the pattern of my childhood insecurity, wanting to be accepted so much by others. I had never put the two together.

As God showed me my weakness, I released it. He started to make me whole, and He healed my insecurity. It didn't happen overnight. But He did heal it!

If He hadn't healed it, I'd probably be the head of the garden club, the women's club and the Junior League—still trying to prove to the world that I am worth something, trying to find acceptance.

I'm not saying there's anything wrong with being the head of organizations. But I needed to look at the *motive* behind it.

When I was about ten years old, some little girl walked right up to me and said, "Carolyn, you're fat." Since she said it, I believed it. But actually I looked like a bean pole. Every picture of me in our family photo album for two years afterward shows me with my arm hiding my "fat" waist.

A form of peer pressure is applied in a lot of marriages. One partner feels insecure because the other one is verbally demeaning him. The insecure partner believes everything the spouse says. When I counsel with insecure persons, I remind them that someone saying something doesn't make it true. We tend to blame ourselves and believe someone else's opinion of us.

Joyce Landorf has written a book entitled *Irregular People*. In it she writes about an irregular person in her life—a person who feels that whatever Joyce does is wrong.

You see, a rational mind cannot understand what an irrational mind is thinking. If you are trying to look at a situation rationally, the other person views it through emotional turmoil. That's the time to pray and ask God to show you what you need to do.

The person with poor self-esteem accepts the "irregular" person's problem as his or her own. I talked with a man once whose wife had left him. He insisted, "It's all my fault. It's got to be my fault. It couldn't possibly be hers. I just did everything wrong."

As he poured out his story, I couldn't find a whole lot he had done wrong. He was so insecure in who he was that he was sure it was all his fault.

Stay Away From Me

As a young girl hurt in peer pressure situations, I was too insecure to stand up for myself. A classmate would say something that hurt me and I would be reduced to tears. At home, I'd tell my mother. She would hurt for me and advise me, "Carolyn, next time someone says that, then you say this."

I'd rehearse her reply, practice it and plan it. But of course no two situations happen exactly the same way. No one ever said exactly the same thing to me. A girl would say something else offensive to me, and, again, I'd be tearful and at a loss for words.

It's important to remember that people who put you down usually feel insecure about themselves. The person leveling rejection at someone does so because of his own feelings of inferiority. Rejection of others is a smoke screen. Insecurity and rejection say, "If I can bring you down to my level, then I won't feel so bad about who I am. I'm going to talk about your problems and faults, then I won't have to deal with mine."

John and I have tried to teach our three children to understand these situations. Often one of them, especially our daughter, will come home from school and report, "So-and-so said this about me."

I'll reply, "Why do you suppose she needed to put you down like that?"

The children are learning. Julie usually says, "She probably doesn't feel very good about herself. If she felt good about herself, why in the world would she need to put somebody else down?"

One day a boy from Julianne's school class was a member of the soccer team against which she was playing. During their game, she came off the field declaring, "I'm so mad at that Teddy. He kicked me. He tripped me. He told me I'm a horrible soccer player. He says I'm no good." She was just devastated.

After acknowledging that I understood how she felt I asked her, "Now why do you suppose Teddy did that?" I asked her.

Julianne responded, "Well, I don't think he likes himself."

I pointed out how Teddy was always getting into trouble at school. "He doesn't have any friends. He doesn't make good grades or seem accepted for anything." Poor Teddy didn't have much going for him, but there was one thing Teddy could do. He could play soccer. "Because Teddy doesn't feel very good about himself, he needs to tell you you're a bad player." I added, "Let's try an experiment. You go to school tomorrow and every time you are around Teddy you tell him what a terrific soccer player he is. Every time you get the chance, you tell him, 'Teddy, you played a great game yesterday. That team could never have won without you!' You do that and see what happens." Julianne looked at me as if I were crazy but shrugged her shoulders and agreed to give it a try.

The next day she came home from school and said, "Mom, it worked! Teddy was nice to me today." I want you to know it was the last time he ever criticized her about anything again. All the kid needed was a little building up.

An older kid in our neighborhood, the neighborhood bully, has threatened my son Randy several times. My growing teenager is no match for this kid in size. One day, he approached Randy to make good his threats. Randy came into the house shaking. I went outside immediately, called the kid over and demanded, "What's the problem?"

Shuffling his feet and laughing, he made some snide remarks. I kept insisting, "What's the problem?"

Finally, he admitted there wasn't any problem

or any reason to bully Randy. I looked that boy straight in the eye and said, "You know, when someone acts like a bully, they're saying, 'I don't feel very good about who I am inside, so I'm going to put up a front to make you think I'm great.'"

Hearing those words caused every bit of the color to drain from that kid's face. The laughter was gone and he grew wide-eyed. I had stripped off his "tough guy" mask and he knew it.

Leaving him in that position would have been damaging, so I added quickly, "I bet if you would relax and be yourself you would find there is a really neat kid inside." Our conversation ended with my restating that point repeatedly using different words. I hoped he would go home with that thought ringing in his ears. I never saw him bully anyone again.

Ever since that day, I have been praying that God would show the boy that he's all right, to heal those insecurities that caused the tough-guy mask.

I Like Who I Am

When people feel good about who they are, they don't have to prove it to anybody else. I was seated on the platform with a speaker one time. It took the person introducing her thirty minutes to read a mile-long list of the woman's credentials and accomplishments.

By the time the introduction concluded, I was sitting there thinking, *Give me a break.* The credentials and accomplishments were great, but hearing all of them didn't do one thing for anybody sitting in the audience.

Watch for people who talk about themselves all the time, telling how great they are. You can be pretty sure they are insecure people—with poor self-esteem.

On the other hand are the people who are comfortable with who they are, and we parents can have a great deal of positive effect on the way our children view themselves.

The seniors in the school my children attend conducted a survey in the kindergarten class. They designed a questionnaire for the young children and wrote their answers for them. Then the answer sheets were sent home.

One question concerned their self-concept: "What am I like?" Most of the other children said things like: "I have brown hair." "I have curly hair." "I have big eyes." "I'm tall—or I'm short." Andrew's answer was "I'm sweet and lovable."

I thought, *Isn't that cute!* Later that day, I caught myself giving him a hug and heard myself saying what I always say, "Andrew, you are so sweet, and I love you."

That's where he got it, I thought. His self-concept came from my repeating that line.

Lest you think I qualify as "Mother of the Year," let me tell you his answer to the question, "What color reminds you of your mother's cooking?" What's the one color every mother would not want her child to name? Yes, he chose black. I thought I was a good cook; but, as a mother, I guess we all have areas on which we're still working.

Last summer when we went to the beach, we

met the family next door. Andrew started playing with their little boy at the beach, and one day John took them on a wildlife excursion to nearby Turtle Mound. Driving along, John heard a conversation between the two boys in the back seat.

The little boy who had no Christian background said to Andrew, "I am really into hard rock."

Andrew responded in his deep voice, "Yeah"—even though he didn't have any idea what hard rock was.

"I really like brass and heavy metal," the boy continued.

Andrew echoed, "Yeah, me too...and my favorite song is 'El Shaddai.' "

The other kid chimed in, "Yeah."

"And my favorite singer is Amy Grant," Andrew added. He had named a contemporary gospel singer and one of her songs that the other boy probably had never even heard of.

John laughed when he told me the story. "Andrew is so secure in his own world; it never occurs to him that he might be in a world totally separate from someone else's."

I guess I feel that same security in my marriage. John tells me, "Carolyn, you say things with such authority that even when I know you are wrong, I'm fooled and think you're right." He bought me a plaque that reads, "Sometimes wrong, but never in doubt."

Deflecting the Arrows

Feeling secure about ourselves does not necessarily mean our emotional structure is whole. If you don't have a problem with insecurity, that's wonderful, but you may still struggle by feeling the brunt of someone else's rejection.

When rejection comes at us, we must pray, "Lord, show me what it is that this person needs. Help her, Lord." That's hard to do because rejection is painful.

For years someone in my life thought whatever I did was wrong. If I stood on my left foot, I should have stood on my right foot. If I gave her a present, I was too materialistic. If I didn't, I wasn't thoughtful. *What am I doing wrong?* I asked myself for a long time. *Why can't I do anything right in this relationship?* I finally came to the realization that I did not own the problem; it belonged to her.

When you get to that point, do what you can and then lay it down. In my situation, I phoned the woman and asked her to tell me everything she could think of that I had ever done to offend her. She gave me a long list.

After naming each offense, I responded, "Would you forgive me?"

She answered, "All right."

At the end of her list, I asked, "Is there anything else you can think of?"

"Yes, there is this and this."

With everything listed and forgiven, I requested, "Can we start our relationship over again?"

"Yes, we can," she agreed.

No, we couldn't. Why? Because the problem was still there. Her emotional insecurity was still separating us. I knew in my heart that I had done everything I could, but that didn't stop me from praying for her. Discovering that she owned the problem brought release into my life. Years later, she understood her insecurity, and the relationship is now on the mend.

We Are Precious in His Sight

God made each one of us unique and precious for what He desires us to do. He wants to dwell in us. We are not made of inferior material, because He doesn't make junk. Our feelings of unworthiness or inferiority are Satan's lies to us.

If rejection has been a problem in your life, dwell on Psalm 139. Let it be the balm that helps heal the feelings that cause you to reject others. The psalm will remind you how much God loves you.

But God is the rebuilder of damaged self-esteem. He wants us to have a healthy love and respect for ourselves. One of my favorite scriptures is Isaiah 61:1: "The Spirit of the Lord God is upon me; because the Lord hath anointed me to preach good tidings unto the meek; he hath sent me to bind up the brokenhearted."

God does bind up the brokenhearted. He heals our emotional wounds of insecurity and rejection. Believe me, He does it; just ask Him to.

Assignment for Living

1. Meditate on the following scriptures to battle insecurity and rejection: Isaiah 61:1; Proverbs 18:10; 1 John 4:4; Psalms 16:5; 3:3; 18:1-3.
2. Talk to God about these questions:
   a. What are the areas where I feel insecure?
   b. Where and why did they start?
   c. Where did the rejection I experienced as a child make its mark?
   d. How do I mask feelings of insecurity?
   e. Do I have a good self-image?
   f. Did peer pressure add to my insecurity?
3. As you read the Word, meditate and ask God to make you whole, I hope you will allow Him to show you your insecure, rejected areas. As it says in Isaiah 61:1, He was sent to bind up the brokenhearted and that includes your own wounded heart. Remember: God doesn't make junk and He wants you to accept who you are. It's OK to like yourself. He wants you to! Ask God to show you yourself as He sees you.
4. Pray this prayer: Dear Lord, Thank You for loving me so unconditionally. Thank you for wanting me even when I don't want myself. Help me reach beyond my distorted opinion of myself and see me as You do. Help me accept who I am. Please, Lord, show me those insecure, rejected places of pain and heal those bleeding places. Let me feel that soothing healing power as I accept Your love for me. I choose to trust You, Lord; You are the feeling-changer. I love You. Amen.

SIX

Handling Guilt

When we were dating in college, John and I went through a traumatic experience. In his junior year he was elected president of the student body at Florida State University. Following the election, he felt burned out from campaigning. He'd let his school work slide, but deadlines were deadlines. He had a paper due in a creative writing class and not enough time to do the work as he should, so he plagiarized from another source.

From the moment John turned the assignment in, he felt guilty. As student body president, he had taken an oath to uphold the student honor system. After much consideration, he confessed his wrongdoing and turned himself in to the chief justice of the honor system.

His confession created quite a stir at the

university: The student body president was kicked out of school. As his steady girlfriend, I supported his decision to confess and stood by him through the whole experience.

False Guilt

Guilt can either be real or false. We feel real guilt when we have walked in sin and need to repent; we know we have done something wrong. But false guilt can hit just as hard as the real thing; it comes from accepting the blame for some wrong we haven't committed.

Although John had cleared his conscience of real guilt, he still contended with feelings of false guilt which stemmed from reactions by his peers. Some friends wondered why John had been so naive or stupid to admit his guilt. Others didn't believe his story and suggested he was kicked out for doing something much worse.

John felt no-good and couldn't forgive himself. Here was a young man with an excellent academic record who felt one mistake had ruined his entire future. His feelings of low self-esteem made it hard for him to let me stand by him through it all.

Guilt makes us feel unacceptable to others as well as ourselves. It drives a wedge between us and the ones we love, but we need each other in those tough times. We tend to pull away—to isolate ourselves to justify our unworthiness.

Since false guilt makes you feel as if you have to "prove yourself worthy," John tried and succeeded. He reapplied for admittance to the university and completed his senior year with a perfect academic record. He was elected president of his fraternity, named to the student "Hall of Fame" and graduated in the top of his class—trying to prove his worth to himself and his peers. But it was not in those accomplishments that he overcame false guilt.

He overcame that false guilt by drawing closer to God. He realized that a "clean slate" comes only from God, no matter what anyone else thinks. His attitude changed to "God, You accept me the way I am whether I accept myself or others accept me."

But, in later years, John had to work through the false guilt again. Whenever he heard sermons about commitment, about being more involved, pressing on, getting more committed, John would come home heavyhearted. He was sure he wasn't doing enough for the Lord when actually he was overcommitted, serving as a Sunday school teacher, leading a fellowship group, counseling, traveling, and speaking about his book, meeting with Christian attorneys and judges...ad infinitum.

This kind of false guilt causes many Christians to do more and more for the Lord, all the while spending less and less personal time with Him. We spent many a frustrating Sunday driving home from church as John focused on needing to do more. "Why," I would ask, "can't you ask God what to do? He doesn't mean for you to be overextended. You can't do it all."

One such time he threw up his hands and said, "I have a teenager in a 'blue-funk' (as we called moodiness); I have another teenager who vacillates between tears and hilarious laughter and a younger son with the tenacity of a bulldozer. I feel as if I'm going through midlife crisis. And I have a pastor who expects me to accomplish 'Mission Impossible'!''

But it was the pastor himself who helped John through his false guilt. We attend a very large church, and the pastor explained to John that he constantly gives challenges for involvement because there are many who don't do anything. The pastor had to say specifically, ''When I give those challenges to commitment, I'm not talking to you, John,'' before John got the point. Even so, periodically, John has to check himself because, the truth is, he would like to do it all! A need is not necessarily a call. Many of us who have this rescuer complex think we are going to save the world all by ourselves and find ourselves overextended and fragmented, unable to do what God has planned for us to do.

My life used to be this way. In the church we formerly attended, I participated in every class and served on every committee. The only church organization I wasn't a member of was the men's club. I remember leaving committee meetings wondering if it was worth it and thinking, *God, are You sure this is what You want me to do?* I was so caught up in my own good works that I couldn't hear Him say no. Then as I became more and more stretched God dealt with me about priorities.

In Acts 1:8 Jesus promised power to the believers and said, ''And ye shall be witnesses unto me both in Jerusalem, and in all Judea, and in

Samaria, and unto the uttermost part of the earth.''
He showed me that the Jerusalem of my life is the
very heart of God, that part dearest to Him, my
own relationship with my loving heavenly Father.
That's not works. It's the time I have with Him—
that moment-by-moment walk as I read His Word,
meditate, pray and listen to His voice. I realized
that I had been so busy running, I hadn't had time
to do any listening!

Next was Judea—the area surrounding Jerusalem. After my relationship to God I was respon-
sible for what He had placed around me—my
family: their needs and our growth together. The
greatest call He had placed on my life was my relationship with John and my responsibility to our
three children.

Then, and only then, came Samaria—the other
things God would call me to do for Him. I wish
we as Christians could see how often we put
Samaria in first place, believing we're doing God's
best and wondering why our lives are so fragmented and unfulfilled. This new understanding
gave me the strength I needed to put my priorities
in order. It's still an ongoing process requiring fre-
quent evaluation, but freedom from the driving
force of false guilt leads to a more balanced Christian walk. False guilt insures a defeated Christian
life. It must be forgotten. But what about real guilt,
which comes from sin? It must be forgiven.

Condemnation vs. Conviction

Remember that false guilt causes condemnation
and real guilt causes conviction, and they
shouldn't be handled the same way. There is such

a difference between the biting sting of condemnation and the gentle yet firm surety of conviction. Everett L. Fullam writes in his book *Riding the Wind*,

> Whenever we feel this correcting, counseling conviction, we're asked to confess our sin. The book of 1 John—again, written to Christians—says: "If we confess our sins, he is faithful and just, and will forgive our sins and cleanse us from all unrighteousness...My little children, I am writing this to you so that you may not sin; but if any one does sin, we have an advocate with the Father, Jesus Christ the righteous."
>
> What does the word "confess" mean? It involves agreeing with the convicting Spirit— saying, "Yes, You're right. I was wrong, and I'm sorry"—then turning back toward the truth and asking forgiveness.[1]

The Holy Spirit doesn't pounce on us with defeating blows, that condemning voice that only adds to the negative opinion we have of ourselves. Rather it's the gentle knowing that comes from God. It convicts our spirits of the sin in our lives and leads us to repentance. We often bring false guilt on ourselves through doctrinal teachings. Paul admonished the Colossians: "So don't let anyone criticize you for what you eat or drink, or for not celebrating Jewish holidays and feasts or new moon ceremonies or Sabbaths. For these were only temporary rules that ended when Christ came" (2:16, TLB).

What bondage so many Christians carry because

of the heavy load of rules and regulations—trying *so* hard to please God with enough good works to be acceptable to Him. That kind of false guilt brings harsh condemnation, self-righteous judgment and a pious facade for "obeying" the rules, when in reality there is no joy, no freedom and no relationship with a loving Father who wants to set us free from the burdensome false guilt we have picked up and carried. Paul is reminding us that Christ came to free us from the law we could never live up to. His grace and mercy set us free. What a difference between false guilt that condemns and the sin of real guilt that convicts our hearts.

Look at the story of Peter who felt deep remorse for denying Jesus after His arrest. Peter had said he would never deny Him—God incarnate whom he had followed for three years, the One who performed miracles, compassionately healed the sick, the Messiah, the Savior. Yet Peter denied even knowing Him, not just once but three times. When reality sank in, the Bible says that "Peter went out and wept bitterly" (Matt. 26:75). Eventually this same Peter who repented felt God's healing forgiveness and went on to be a dynamic force in furthering the kingdom of God. He didn't stay under the burden of guilt; repentance brings forgiveness and freedom.

I too have felt the guilt of denying Christ in my unloving attitudes and critical comments, especially to my husband and children. Recently I was helping my daughter with her homework. I was frustrated because she didn't understand a basic point in math, and finally I said, "What is this—do we need to go back to second grade?" The minute that critical remark came out of my mouth I knew it was wrong. Here I was, the one who majored in child development in college, who teaches on the importance of building good self-esteem, and I had asked my teenager if we needed to go back to second grade! You know what's even worse? I had a check about saying it before it came out, and I said it anyway!

Julianne looked at me sadly and said, "Mother, that didn't do any good." Not only had I denied the God I serve, but I had denied Julianne her self-respect. Yes, I repented and asked forgiveness and God restored us both, but if the guilt for real sin is not confessed and forgiven, it will be punished.

Self-Punishment

We must seek forgiveness from God for sin or God will punish us, and we will find a way to punish ourselves.

In the previous chapter, I told you the tragic story of a young man with a failure complex who committed suicide. This story had a dramatic impact on a guilt-ridden young woman in jail after her second arrest for prostitution. God gave me an opportunity to speak to the female inmates in the local jail where she was being held.

John had spoken at the chapel before and accompanied me. Though the correctional facilities were familiar territory to him, having visited clients in jail, I'd never visited inmates. No one had told me they couldn't have pencils. (I almost asked them to take notes.) No one had told me I shouldn't ask why they were in jail. (Fortunately I'd decided not to ask.)

John spoke to the male inmates, and two men accepted Jesus. Then it was my turn to speak to the women. It just so happened that the air conditioner was broken. The prayer team was praising God, declaring they didn't feel the heat. I wondered where they were getting their air because I was burning up! The group was crowded into a hot, stuffy cafeteria, and, as I spoke, everyone was waving arms and fans for relief from the heat. On top of the high temperature, an intercom blared, repeatedly interrupting me.

Despite the distractions, the women listened attentively. I felt led of the Lord to tell about the young man's life and death to emphasize how God reaches out in love. His story showed how God tried to get his attention to let him know life was worth living.

After the service, the young woman convicted of prostitution came to a counselor. The woman was to be released from jail the next day. But the guilt she carried about her way of living was more than she could handle; she'd decided to punish herself. "I've been asking God all day long if it would be all right for me to take my life. The thought of getting out of here and going back to the streets was so horrible. But now I know I can't take my life," she sobbed.

She confessed her sin and received that soothing, healing forgiveness, that cleansing that comes only from God. The counselor got some help for her from rehabilitation agencies. The realization that God does care and the willingness of people to help her gave the young woman a new start on a better life.

We need to secure God's forgiveness, but we also need to forgive ourselves. Sometimes we accept the fact that God has forgiven us much easier than we can forgive ourselves. I believe the inability to do this often stems from trying to live up to the image we create for others to see—that perfect, always loving, kind person who doesn't make mistakes. Trying to be perfect makes it difficult to forgive ourselves for making an error. Letting down those walls we must simply admit our sin, confess it, accept it as truth and repent. Accept the loving forgiveness of God and accept yourself. You may need to repeat this process over and over, depending on whether or not you will accept God's cleansing and believe He really does what He says. Isaiah 1:18 reads, "Come now, and let us reason together, saith the Lord: though your sins be as scarlet, they shall be as white as snow; though they be red like crimson, they shall be as wool."

If we suppress our guilt, it may breed illness or some act of volatile anger. It doesn't go away unless it is resolved. I have seen people severely criticize the sin in another person's life, only to find later they had been guilty of the same wrong. They were raging over the atrocity of someone else's sin in an effort to cover their own. That Shakespearean quote, "Me thinks thou dost protest too much," is often true as we attempt to assuage our guilt and cover sin.

If we don't resolve guilt by receiving God's forgiveness and forgiving ourselves, we internalize our guilt which can manifest itself in the form of depression, despondency, moodiness or remorse. It is also a well-known fact that actual physical illness can emerge from emotional trauma.

That's why Jesus asked the man who was sick, "Wilt thou be made whole?" (John 5:6). When Jesus talked about *wholeness*, He referred to more than physical healing.

When Jesus healed bodies, He would say, "Your sins be forgiven." Why do you suppose He did that? He was healing emotional structures as well as physical bodies. In Matthew 9 we read,

And, behold, they brought to him a man sick of the palsy, lying on a bed: and Jesus seeing their faith said unto the sick of the palsy; Son, be of good cheer; thy sins be forgiven thee. And, behold, certain of the scribes said within themselves, This man blasphemeth. And Jesus knowing their thoughts said, Wherefore think ye evil in your hearts?

For whether is easier, to say, Thy sins be forgiven thee; or to say, Arise and walk? But that ye may know that the Son of man hath power on earth to forgive sins, (then saith he to the sick of the palsy,) Arise, take up thy bed, and go unto thine house" (vv. 2-6).

The first thing Jesus did was forgive the man's sins, healing his guilt and blotting his wrongdoing from God's record. Many times we focus more on the physical healing without realizing that Jesus has another great work to do. He wants to heal the emotional structures inside our bodies.

Confess to One Another

Guilt must be expressed through the verbal means of confession. That's why the Bible says, "Confess your faults one to another...that ye may be healed" (James 5:16). There's cleansing in confessing your faults. Recently my son's basketball team had an exciting, tension-packed game with its main rival. The score was close the entire evening, and John and I are what you might call "energetic" fans. The referee seemed to favor the other team, calling us for every foul and ignoring many of theirs.

We lost by one point, and as we walked out of the gym I said in a rather upset loud voice, "That was the poorest refereed game I've ever seen!" When I looked up, not two yards in front of me stood the referee! We walked in silence to the car. Would you believe we were parked right next to each other, and it seemed like ages before John unlocked the door to let me in. I was so embarrassed. At the next basketball game I told several friends what I had done. Somehow the good medicine of confession helped me over the hump of my big mouth. And those precious people not only accepted my weakness but admitted similar situations of their own.

Whether we do the confessing or hear someone else's confessions, woe be unto us if we don't respond as God would have us. No one has the right to listen with a judgmental attitude to a confession of a weakness or problem. This is no time for advice giving but rather a time for acceptance and forgiveness.

Stop and think about those things in your life that make you feel guilty. Do you feel a conviction of sin? Do you need to ask sincerely for the Father's forgiveness? Is there a need for genuine repentance? If so, He will forgive, but repentance means turning around and walking away from sin.

Repentance demands true sincerity, not just lip service. God says He removes sin and remembers it no more. Psalm 103:12 says, "As far as the east is from the west, so far hath he removed our transgressions from us."

If there's no sin in your life, then let God show you the reason you feel so condemned. Who or what is bringing condemnation on you? Once God reveals the source, He can heal your guilt.

Assignment for Living

1. Meditate on these scriptures regarding false guilt: James 5:16; Psalm 103:12; Romans 8:1; Job 27:6.
2. Ask God to make the answers to these questions clear to you.
   a. In what areas of my life do I feel guilty?
   b. Does the guilt I feel convict or condemn me?
   c. Do I suffer from false guilt because I don't "do enough" for God? Am I works oriented?
   d. In what areas do I need to confess sin?
   e. Can I accept God's forgiveness?
   f. Can I forgive myself?
3. Separating real and false guilt can be tremendously freeing. Recognizing false guilt, understanding its origin and laying it down will bring a release. Continue to walk that out by meditating on His Word and refusing those imaginations (see 2 Cor. 10:5). Recognize who wants to put false guilt back on you and refuse it. Draw near to God and the devil has to flee!

   Recognizing real guilt will also bring freedom as you confess the sin, repent before a Father who loves you and accept His forgiveness. Forgiving yourself becomes possible as you accept God's love and forgiveness for you. It's a trick of the enemy to browbeat you with your past. Once you've repented and walked the other way, God removes your sin as far as the east is from the west.

He said it, so I believe it!

4. Pray the following prayer: Dear God, I praise You that You are the one who gives discernment to Your children. Please show me, Lord, areas of guilt in my life. Make clear to me those areas where I need to repent and ask Your forgiveness. And show me where I have assumed false guilt. Help me to lay that down and walk in Your freedom. All-knowing, all-wise Father, I thank You for loving me into wholeness. Help me accept this freedom with joy, free from the bondage of a guilty spirit. I love You, Lord. Thank You for Your goodness. Amen.

SEVEN

Freedom From Anxiety

Anxiety can be defined as inner conflict. When it permeates our lives and destroys our peace, it renders us ineffective. We need to ask God to reveal the source and heal the wound.

I shared with you earlier about the anxiety I felt in social situations because of the insecurity from being rejected by my peers as a child. Although God revealed that to me and healed it, I recently found that the anxiety had influenced my attitudes about my children's relationships. I noticed how sensitive I was when they talked about their friends' activities. I'd quickly ask my children if they were invited or included or what the other kids were doing. I identified my anxiety over not wanting them to be left out—not wanting them

97

to be hurt as I had been. Strangely enough, God revealed this to me through my own children. I noticed that they were unaffected by the times they weren't included and often chose to make their own plans. As I released this inner feeling prayerfully, I thanked God for their self-esteem.

Anxiety over acceptance affects so many people. I counseled a woman recently so laden with anxiety over rejection that she could not give me eye contact. She stared at my neck as she poured out her feelings. Her problems focused around what others thought of her and she was constantly evaluating their opinions of her actions. It hurts to see people ridden with anxiety. I know other people this way. They are so jammed up they can barely carry on a conversation, often turning their heads away and looking for a way of escape. It keeps us from being vulnerable when we're so concerned with what others think of us. We can't be real—that might not be acceptable.

Anxiety is often a by-product of a deeper wound. Rejection, insecurity, feelings of inferiority, guilt or fear carry anxiety with them. So many are interrelated, like the tentacles of an octopus as they wrap one by one around our lives in an effort to destroy our peace and progress into wholeness.

I once spoke with a woman who had been molested as a child. She had never confided in anyone because she felt that such things were the child's fault. Her feelings of false guilt stifled her relationships with men, particularly her husband. Her resentment toward men fed the anxiety deep within her. Her confession was the beginning of her walk to wholeness. She is now getting counseling and releasing these feelings so God can heal the wounds and scars hidden for so long.

Anxiety also is produced in love-hate relationships. Many unresolved marriage conflicts are based in this kind of interaction. In our home we have a miniature dachshund, Munchkin, who displays anxiety in just such a relationship.

He has tremendous love and hate for our new golden retriever, Trooper. Usually the dachshund loves the ground the retriever walks on, cuddling up next to him to sleep, seeking him out wherever he goes. But woe be unto that retriever if he takes a toy—any toy—to chew on. Munchkin wants it, wants all the possessions, attention and food, hungry or not. I've seen him guard a piece of stale pizza (which he had no intention of eating) for two hours just so Trooper couldn't have it. It's a stitch to watch him hate the dog he loves so much!

Sadly, however, we humans display the same kind of inner conflict. There are things about people that we can't stand, yet we are intensely in love with them. Those love-hate relationships are another example of anxiety, which permeates more of our lives than we are willing to admit.

Anxiety not understood and dealt with will find a way of expression. One of my son's teenage friends wears his "I'm cool" mask to hide the anxiety he feels over his rejection by girls. He is constantly talking about all the girls he's met and how impressed they are with him. It's all an attempt to mask the anxiety he feels inside.

Bert Ghezzi writes in *Transforming Problems*, "When I was a teenager, there was nothing I wanted more than to succeed at sports. However, I was small, uncoordinated, and performed poorly in every event I tried. My failure hurt a lot, but I pretended not to care. I thrust myself into academics and public speaking, at which I excelled. I worked at giving the impression that somehow sports were beneath me, and this pose masked my disappointment with myself."[1] Notice the statement, "I pretended not to care." So he masked his anxiety with the superior front of being above sports. Often the facade of pride or arrogance masks anxiety. We puff ourselves up outwardly to cloud how low we actually feel about ourselves inside.

Denying Anxiety

The anxiety that builds up in us can be handled in one of several ways. First of all, we can deny it. Many times we unconsciously ignore the fact that anxiety is within us, and we push it down like a jack-in-the-box. But it may spring up at any minute.

Invariably when I'm in a time crunch I get anxious. My melancholy temperament is organized and prompt. Being late isn't part of my agenda and when I run out of time, anxiety creeps in. John, on the other hand, never thinks he's late. I once reminded him he was supposed to pick up the babysitter at 6:30. "No problem," he quipped, "I'll be on time." It was then 6:45! In my efforts to become less controlled by the clock I will deny my anxiety, trying to control it. But my perceptive husband will often say, "Carolyn, just relax," to which I've snapped back, "I *am* relaxed." My tone of voice has given me away, my efforts to deny anxiety obviously exposed.

Avoiding Anxiety

Second, we can avoid anxiety. A shy person might avoid being in a crowd or a person with a fear of heights might avoid high places. The anxiety is restrained as long as we can stay far away from any situation that might churn up any turmoil.

I know a person who avoids anxiety by switching churches, jobs and friends. She is so insecure and has such a low opinion of herself that she fears anyone knowing her well. They might find her unacceptable. As soon as she starts to become involved with people, the anxiety over possible rejection wells up and she pulls away. She has left behind her a trail of broken relationships, short-lived jobs and church stints. There is always something wrong with all those people. This illustrates avoiding anxiety as well as rationalizing it.

Rationalizing Anxiety

Third, we unconsciously rationalize anxiety. Cecil Osborne tells a personal experience about rationalizing anxiety. It demonstrates the difference between asking God to change you and letting Him show you why you need to change. Remember, He wants to reveal, then heal.

Osborne explains that he always sets out to accomplish a long list of tasks at his office each day. One particular day, he was having a hard time getting anything done because of constant interruptions. While counseling a woman, he realized how tense and uptight he was about his unfinished work. He knew the woman and his staff members were sensing his anxiety, as he was being somewhat irritable.

Later that day, Osborne examined his feelings toward the woman and his staff. He realized the *real* problem. He writes,

Then I saw that I had been rationalizing my anxiety. I had attributed it to my zeal to finish the task, and a consequent sense of failure if I did not manage to achieve all I had outlined for myself.

As a child, I had felt acceptable to my parents only when I had performed my tasks well and on time. Now as an adult I found that I could accept myself only if I had finished my self-appointed tasks on time. I felt vaguely guilty and inadequate when I did not. There was no parent to criticize, except the "parent within," who resides in each of us.

My guilt feelings did not, in any sense, constitute "real guilt"; they were "false guilt." I was guilty only before the accusing conscience, conditioned by childhood. By a series of clever rationalizations I had managed to make a virtue (of accomplishing all these things on time)....The task I then set for myself was to insist that the adult of the present make decisions instead of the inner child of the past.[2]

We can rationalize our anxiety and never really get to the root of why it's there. God needs to *reveal* before He heals.

Narcotizing Our Anxiety

Fourth, we narcotize anxiety. Many people narcotize their problems, literally, with drugs and alcohol. But there are other ways to narcotize anxiety. A compulsive worker falls into this category.

I once knew a woman who volunteered for everything. She was team mother for all the sports, room mother, church worker, Sunday school teacher, lunchroom volunteer and on and on. She loved to talk about her endless activities, how she never had enough time to get it all done but after all, "If you want a job done, ask a busy person." How many times have you heard that one! But compulsive workers are hiding something in an effort to narcotize anxiety. In this case, communication with her husband had stopped. The marriage was in real trouble. Her husband was spending more and more time at the office to narcotize his own anxiety. This relationship was a disaster waiting to happen.

Others engage in a fast pace of social activities to keep busy. These people aren't necessarily socially minded but escaping from the anxiety of being alone. Whether it's excessive partying or "good works" at church, these compulsive efforts narcotize the gentle voice of God drawing us to examine the anxious feelings that keep us separated from ourselves and that wholeness to which God calls us.

Children have humorous ways of narcotizing their anxiety. When Julie was little and about to get a spanking, she would plead, "Wait a minute,

Mommy.'' Then my daughter would run upstairs to her room and put on six pairs of panties. The extra layers of clothing were her attempt to narcotize the anxiety of her spanking.

Andrew did something similar to narcotize his anxiety about a doctor's visit. He needed to go for his check-up but was anxious about whether he'd be given a shot. I assured him there'd be no need for an injection.

Andrew asked if he'd have his finger pricked. I answered him honestly, admitting that the nurse would probably prick his finger for a blood test. I then offered him the consolation that the prick would hardly hurt. He moaned and groaned about it anyway, and I promised that I'd buy him a treat after his check-up—if he'd not complain and accept the fact that he had to go. He didn't mention his apprehension again. But the next morning when he got ready to go to the doctor's office, Andrew put on his sneakers, shorts and shirt—appropriate for the summertime weather—and his red winter gloves. He hoped they would keep the needles away, and they helped narcotize the pain of his anxiety!

Getting to the Source

The fifth and only effective way to deal with anxiety is to ask God to reveal and heal the source of it. Often the roots go down deep into our unconscious. Remember that the One who loves us best also knows the most about us.

John is so loving and caring about people. He can sit down and deal with somebody's problem in the midst of chaos and not be distracted. On the other hand, I'm such an organizer. I want to get all my little ducks in order, have everything lined up before turning my attention to others. I'm always thinking about what I need to be doing to keep on schedule.

"God, I want to be more like John," I prayed. "I want to think about other people and forget all the things that need to be done." And God showed me that, even though organization was part of my temperament, I was also repeating a childhood pattern: I felt I had to accomplish something tangible to be worthy.

I had been rationalizing the anxiety I felt (over lack of accomplishment) as being part of my organized temperament that likes to follow schedules and set priorities in order. As a child I had watched my mother always busy, always getting a great deal accomplished and seldom relaxing. She was the oldest of five children, always given much responsibility that didn't stop when she reached adulthood. She'd had an endless stream of relatives to care for. There was never, and still isn't, any time for her to do just what she wanted. I accepted that as a measure of my real value. What did relaxing achieve? Nothing, as far as I could see. As God showed me the origins of this anxiety over accomplishment, He dealt with me about my feelings of unworthiness. I actually didn't feel I deserved time for just me. Honestly, I'm still grappling with this one. The healing process is sometimes slow, but it's possible, and God does heal these wounds infected by anxiety.

Scriptures help us as we search out anxiety and

deal with it. Psalm 37:5 states, "Commit thy way unto the Lord; trust also in him; and he shall bring it to pass." Repeating that verse will be an antidote for the anxiety you feel.

Other verses that provide medicine for inner conflict include Psalm 55:22, "Cast thy burden upon the Lord and he shall sustain thee: he shall never suffer the righteous to be moved," and Proverbs 16:3, "Commit thy works unto the Lord and thy thoughts shall be established."

When feelings of anxiety creep in, I combat them with Scripture. As I identify the anxiety, I say conscientiously, "No, I don't need that. The Bible says, 'Trust in the Lord with all thine heart, and lean not unto thine own understanding. In all thy ways acknowledge Him and he shall direct thy paths' (Prov. 3:5,6). Lord, I choose to acknowledge You and the peace You give me in this situation."

God doesn't intend for you to live with anxiety. It's a wound that keeps you from being whole before Him. Let God focus His light on every area of your life and remove your inner conflict.

Assignment for Living

1. To stand against anxiety, meditate on God's Word: Psalms 55:22; 37:5; Proverbs 16:3; 3:5,6; Philippians 4:6; Matthew 6:26-34; Jeremiah 17:7,8.

2. Ask God to help you answer these questions:
   a. Am I aware of anxiety in my life?
   b. What situations make me feel anxious?
   c. Are there wounds in my life causing anxiety? Insecurity? Rejection? Fear? Guilt? Low self-esteem?
   d. How do I deal with my anxiety? Do I deny it? Avoid it? Rationalize it? Narcotize it?

3. As God helps you identify those anxious feelings, ask Him to show you their roots. Understand them; tell Him how you feel and ask Him to heal those anxiety-ridden places in your life. Use the Word as medicine for those wounded spots.

4. Pray: Dear Lord, Thank You for assuring me that I need not be anxious for anything. You've promised to take care of me, and I praise You for Your love and constant watchful eye over me. Lord, help me see those anxious places and allow You to make me whole. Reveal the sources of anxiety that I hide and cause me to seek them out and deal with them. Thank You for being my healer of damaged emotions. Amen.

EIGHT

The Plague of Pride

As college students, John and I, along with a couple of my sorority sisters, rode from Daytona Beach back to Florida State University in Tallahassee after a spring break. John drove. Passing through Jacksonville on the interstate, we came over a hill and saw the toll gate at the Fuller-Warren Bridge.

Once we paid the toll, we crossed the bridge and kept traveling. In a short while, the scenery looked familiar to me. *I've seen this before,* I thought.

Pretty soon, we came over a hill and saw the toll gate and bridge again. "I think we're lost," I commented.

John replied assuredly, "We're not lost. I know exactly what I did wrong. No problem. I've got this under control."

We paid our toll, crossed the bridge again and proceeded down the highway. Before long, I saw familiar signs along the road, only this time I kept quiet.

Then we came over the hill and saw the toll gate again. By now, John was getting a little embarrassed, but he still would not admit he needed directions.

Finally, the fifth time we came over the hill and approached the bridge, the man came out of his toll booth. "Stop," he said, "don't pay this time. Just go on through, and tell me where in the world you're trying to go so you don't come through here again."

John surely isn't alone in his struggle to admit his own humanity, and many times our pride can block our journey to wholeness just as crucially as pride blocked our journey back to campus.

A couple living in another city called me for counseling about their difficult marriage problems. "Why don't you talk to your pastor?" I advised them.

"Oh no, we don't want him to know about this," they insisted.

"How about your Sunday school teacher?" I suggested. I was sure their teacher, who happened to be a good friend of mine, would reach out to them and love them.

"Oh no, we don't want that person to know about this problem," the husband and wife explained.

Finally, I asked them a pointed question. "Do you know that the purpose of the body of Christ is to help you through the problem?"

Pride had separated the couple from the source of help closest to them. Satan had them just where he wanted them, isolated with their problem. Proverbs 16:18 tells how God feels about pride. "Pride goeth before destruction, and a haughty spirit before a fall." In Daniel we find the story of Nebuchadnezzar, king of Babylon, who became puffed up with pride for his achievements, forgetting that God had given him his great kingdom. God warned Nebuchadnezzar through a dream interpreted by Daniel that if Nebuchadnezzar did not stop his sin and show mercy to the poor, he would go insane. In God's mercy He gave the king twelve months to repent and change, but Nebuchadnezzar was filled with his self-righteous pride and refused to listen. According to Daniel 4:30,31:

> The king spake, and said, Is not this great Babylon, that I have built for the house of the kingdom by the might of *my* power, and for the honor of *my* majesty? While the word was in the king's mouth, there fell a voice from heaven, saying, O king Nebuchadnezzar, to thee it is spoken; The kingdom is departed from thee.

That same hour the king went mad. His pride had been his destruction. God can't work in our lives when we're full of our own self-righteousness.

Pride Can Keep Us From Each Other

John and I went to Pennsylvania a few years ago to speak at a conference. As we were preparing to go, God spoke to me about pride. It seemed that every scripture or devotional I read concerned this issue.

I prayed, "Lord, wherever the pride is in my life, please show me. I don't want anything between You and me when I go to Pennsylvania to minister." I asked God over and over to show me my sin. I was so sure I had some hidden pride that I wasn't listening to what the Lord was trying to say to me.

During our flight from Florida, we had to change planes several times. On each airplane, God placed someone beside us who was so tense we could see the uptight look on his face. Each person was talkative and cordial, trying to hide the uneasiness. Our fellow passengers projected images that were easy for us to see through. They were too proud to show us who they really were.

As I saw their pride, the Lord revealed to me why He'd brought pride to my attention. I remembered that the pastor and his wife had told us that the people to whom we were going to minister never shared their problems. "They never talk about anything that's going on in their lives," they'd said. I realized a spirit of pride prevailed among these people, just as it did among our fellow travelers. God was trying to show me what I was going into. And as we circled over the airport, the Holy Spirit instructed me to be open and honest in my presentation. He wanted me to be as vulnerable as I could in front of those people then watch what would happen.

What God did absolutely amazed me. From the time John and I finished speaking until after midnight, the people came to us in a steady stream.

They opened up to us, sharing things for the first time in their lives. They were real and honest about themselves and where they had suffered. Pride had kept them closed up for so long, and pride keeps us closed up.

One woman unleashed the bitterness and resentment she felt for the elderly parents who lived with her. She felt in bondage to their needs and often unappreciated and unloved. She prided herself on her sacrificial role and had shoved the anger she felt deep down as being unacceptable for a Christian. Confessing her feelings did wonders for her outward appearance. By the end of the conference this tight-lipped woman with drawn features seemed relaxed, natural and even smiling.

Although many people give themselves away in demeanor, there was one family I would never have guessed was hiding behind the mask of pride. This young family was vibrant, happy and heavily involved in the church. At the close of the conference, however, the wife approached me cautiously. She poured out her feelings of not feeling free to tell her husband her frustration about their overinvolvement in church activities. The great demands on her as a wife and mother of three small children left her drained with all the other activities.

In the name of submission she felt she had no right to stand in the way of God's work or tell her husband her true feelings. We worked through her own feelings of inadequacy, her resentments and her guilt feelings, and she began to separate what

God was saying to her from her "works oriented" background. Pride had effectively cut off her communication with her husband and with God.

Pride Can Keep Us From God

Pride not only separates us from others, it separates us from God.

When John and I received the baptism of the Holy Spirit, we grew ravenous for the Word of God. The Scriptures came alive to us—especially the verses on divine healing. We believed that Isaiah 53:5, "With his stripes we are healed," meant Christians could live free from sickness and disease.

John went so far as to tell his law partners they needed to drop their group health insurance plan. When the other lawyers refused to change office policy, John canceled our coverage.

We felt we'd received a revelation concerning divine healing that others had failed to accept. In fact, I prided myself on being an authority on the subject of healing.

At the home of friends we excitedly shared "our discovery" of divine health over dinner one evening. "Christians don't have to be sick," John asserted. I amened him.

He pointed out that our son Randy, then two-and-a-half, had never been sick and neither had we—since we'd started to walk in divine health.

All of the people at this particular gathering had been living for the Lord a lot longer than we had, but we felt the need to enlighten them on divine healing. There we sat, with a pastor and his wife as well as the church administrator and his wife, expounding on our newfound spiritual truth.

During the conversation, Randy walked over to the table. The look on his face indicated that he was hurting. "Mom...," he said, and seconds later he threw up all over the floor! John and I excused ourselves and exited the house feeling humiliated. And soon after God confronted me about my pride. It was taking precedence over His love and mercy.

Randy's sickness forced us to adapt our theories on divine health to accommodate illness. But we still believed divine healing was available anytime simply for the asking. We had another lesson to learn about how God heals.

Not long after the dinner table incident, we made plans to attend a football game at our alma mater in Tallahassee. The day before our trip, John came home from work and crawled into bed.

"I am sick. I think I've got the flu. We'll have to forget going to the game," he groaned. For John to miss a football game at FSU meant he really felt bad!

As John crept from the bed to the bathroom on his hands and knees, he earnestly prayed, "God, I'm believing You to heal me." Suddenly, he heard a voice, as clearly as he had ever heard any voice, saying, "Well, then, if I've healed you, what are you doing on the floor?"

Immediately, he stood up and was totally restored physically. He quickly let me know he wanted to go to the game after all. "I feel fine now," he testified.

"Come on. I *know* how much you want to go to the game, but do you really feel well enough?"

I tried to reason with him.

He reaffirmed that he felt fine, and so we drove to Tallahassee.

But as soon as we arrived at our motel, I came down with the flu. Was I ever sick!

John's calculated reaction was, "No problem. I'll open my Bible and lay hands on you. Then you will pop out of that bed and go to the game." He still believed, as I did, that God would do what we said because we asked Him to do it. John prayed for me, but I stayed in the motel bed all weekend, too sick to move.

Through these events, God spoke to us about our haughty spirits and about His sovereignty. He emphasized that while the Scriptures are true, they aren't to be used as formulas to get Him to act at our will. He isn't a personal valet. We needed to trust Him as God and not make decisions for Him or use our doctrinal beliefs to put demands on Him. Had we not listened to God as He chastened us for our haughty spirits, we would have continued in our self-righteousness. Pride, however, affects not only our relationship with God. It spills over and makes us judgmental and condemning of others.

Recently we were at a dinner party with several other couples whom we didn't know well. Soon the conversation turned to an interest shared by everyone but us. John and I listened as they excitedly discussed their involvement. But as the conversation continued, up through the cracks and around the edges seeped the self-righteous voice of pride. All of a sudden, their way became the *only* way; other methods were just not as good or effective and I squirmed because of the air of superiority.

"No," I wanted to say, "there are other good ways too." But it wouldn't have done any good. The pride was so thick, you could cut the air with a knife.

We categorize and separate ourselves from God and others when we fall into the pride trap.

Jesus talked a lot about humility. The Bible says in Isaiah 57:15, "I dwell...with him also that is of a contrite and humble spirit, to revive the spirit of the humble, and to revive the heart of the contrite ones."

God promises to dwell with those who are humble. In 2 Chronicles 7:14 He also promises to heal our land if we will humble ourselves and pray. In James, He talks about resisting the proud, but giving grace to the humble.

How do we cultivate humility? Follow Jesus' example. He was a servant. He was equal with God yet made Himself of no degree to save us—the ultimate in servanthood and humility. Oh that our prayer would be, "I want to be just like You, Lord!"

Has pride kept you from being open and honest about yourself? Has your pride made you feel separated from others and God? If you answered yes to these questions, ask God to remove the plague of pride in your life. Ask Him to show you those areas of judgment and superiority. I know it's not easy—not pretty—but yet it's so necessary to wholeness.

Assignment for Living

1. As you deal with pride meditate on these scriptures: Proverbs 6:16,17; 16:5,18,19; 1 John 2:15-17; James 4:6-10,16; 2 Chronicles 7:14; Isaiah 57:15; Matthew 18:4; 23:12; 1 Peter 5:5,6.
2. Answer these questions prayerfully:
   a. Am I plagued by pride?
   b. Is pride separating me from others? From God?
   c. Do I have a judgmental attitude toward others?
   d. Do I have a humble and contrite spirit?
   e. How does God use me as a servant?
3. Perhaps this is the most difficult of all the areas to deal with, but God has promised freedom if we face it and give it up as we walk in humility before Him. I encourage you to accept God's loving correcting hand if pride is in your life.
4. Pray: Dear Lord, Thank You for Your mercy and loving direction as I face this difficult area of a haughty spirit. I pray for forgiveness and an open eye to see truth. Show me the way out as I lay this ugly mess at your feet. I accept Your healing touch on my life. I love You so much. Amen.

NINE

Deliverance From Fear

When I was a little girl, people used to call me "W.W." Those initials stood for my nickname, Worry Wart. I could always find some reason to worry about something.

On my journey to wholeness, God showed me that fear was at the root of my worry. Little by little, God has delivered me from my fears. Fear of acceptance left as God healed insecurity. Fear of rejection left as God healed feelings of inferiority. Slowly, as God revealed these wounds, and I dared to look, He healed those fearful places.

In one dramatic example, I had an excessive fear of fire that I couldn't overcome. My fear was due, in part, to an incident that happened when I was two years old. I discovered a fire in our kitchen. I remember standing at the kitchen entrance as the whole room seemed a mass of flames. I was filled with terror as I ran screaming for my mother. From then on I had recurring dreams that our house was on fire, and I had only a few moments to save what I wanted.

As an adult, this fear of fire overwhelmed me. I couldn't leave my house with the oven on. I hated fireplaces. (I grew up in a home with four of them and I hated them all.) Every time I drove through the neighborhood and caught a glimpse of our house through the trees, a fearful thought ran through my mind. I was afraid I'd see flames and smoke billowing from our home.

I asked God to take away my fear of fire. I searched the Scriptures for a solution. I needed deliverance from fear. Finally, I experienced complete deliverance by asking others to pray for me. A Spirit-filled believer took authority over my fear in the name of Jesus and commanded it to leave me. The fear of fire has never tormented me again. Praise God for deliverance from fear, not only for me, but for a friend of mine.

Sandy's Story

She called me one day to tell me that the doctor had found a lump in her breast. She was terrified and hardly able to function. "I need prayer, so I'm calling all my prayer partners," she said.

Sandy and I had grown up together, so I could sense the fear in her voice. I told her, "Sandy, ever since I've known you, your whole family has reacted in fear when it comes to a physical ailment."

She replied, "I know. It's the truth. Since I was

a little girl any physical problem, no matter how minor, would arouse my parents' fear. They'd say, 'We need to get that checked right away,' and take me to the doctor. Now every time something happens to me physically, I panic," she confided. Fear virtually paralyzed her day-to-day life.

"Your inability to function is not because of the lump in your breast," I stated. "It's not just a physical problem. It's an emotional problem as well. Fear is keeping you from coping."

Then I added, "I believe God has allowed this physical problem to give you emotional victory. Satan is never going to control you again through fear as he has all your life."

Sandy agreed, declaring, "I believe it!"

We prayed together and fought her fear with the Word of God. She based her fight against fright on 2 Corinthians 10:5 which speaks of "casting down imaginations" and "bringing into captivity every thought to the obedience of Christ."

Every time fear would grip Sandy, she would rebuke it, saying, "No, that is imagination. I cast it down in the name of Jesus. I refuse to entertain that thought. It must come into the obedience of Christ."

The physical problem proved to be nothing serious, no malignancy. And because she fought and won the battle over fear, Satan has not been able to hold her in the grip of fear since. He has tried many times, but she's been victorious over fear each time.

Many of our fears are overcome as we step out into the unknown. In Hannah Hurnard's book

Hinds' Feet on High Places, we meet the character "Much-Afraid," who was led by the Shepherd, Jesus, to the high places of the Spirit. The journey was treacherous at times and many of Much-Afraid's fears were conquered as she stepped out in faith, one step at a time.

Being afraid to entertain or have guests for dinner will become easier the more you do it. As we walk in faith to conquer these fears, they are reduced. I wish you could have seen John and me the first time we appeared on television. Scared is hardly an adequate description of how we felt. There John stood clutching his book in front of him with a half smile pasted on his face as I sat— pale, sweaty palms and a stomach in knots. But the amazing part is that we survived! It really wasn't so bad! Repeating these television appearances has erased the fear we had. It's not frightening at all anymore. In fact, it's fun!

Our Temperaments

So often we encourage fear by dwelling on the negative. I had to learn to be a positive person. A negative perspective on life came naturally to me. Why? Because of my natural temperament.

In his temperament analysis brochure Tim LaHaye teaches: "There is no more powerful influence on your behavior than your inherited temperament. Like the color of your hair, eyes, height, and I.Q., temperament is passed on genetically at conception. Some authorities believe that between 10 and 25 percent of your behavior is the result of your temperament."[1]

Each person has a primary temperament and a

secondary temperament, and the two influence each other. These combinations, along with the other factors that affect who we are, mean no two people are exactly alike. In addition, the dominance of these primary and secondary temperaments can change with one's circumstances.

I've learned that I have a melancholy temperament. What does that mean? A melancholy is a perfectionist-prone, gifted, aesthetic person with a sensitive and conscientious nature who can be moody or critical. Artists, writers and other creative people usually have a melancholy temperament. While they are very organized and introspective, they can fall into worry and depression. I had to fight "I can't" all the way up the mountain of any achievement I ever made. The main obstacle I had to overcome was my negative, fearful attitude that fed the comfort zone of not trying rather than risking failure. I would often try for things beyond my reach, but the anxiety as I reached for new goals was unbelievable. I often wondered if it was worth it.

John has a sanguine temperament. He's a warm, outgoing, friendly person who abounds with so much charisma that he often runs off in several directions at once. My husband never met a stranger. He absolutely loves people. He's positive and upbeat. There's no one more fun to be with than a sanguine temperament, and God smiled on me the day He gave me John. But that same wonderful sanguine sometimes becomes overextended. Too many things to be accomplished in too short a time can cause anxiety and fear of not doing his best.

Fear wraps itself around us in so many ways. It's in those quiet times of hearing from God that we learn how to overcome the weaknesses in our temperaments.

The choleric temperament is that active, hard-driving, goal-oriented, strong, natural leader who has a life-long problem with anger. A person with this personality has the ability to see a goal and head toward it. Often, this is the temperament of the head of a corporation who is trying to achieve success. He may unknowingly step on people in the process of climbing the ladder because of being so goal-oriented. If fear is festering beneath a choleric temperament, it may boost the aggressive force that drives a person causing him to plunge ahead, pell-mell toward a goal, never heeding the gentle voice of the Holy Spirit. It's like the joke about the airline pilot who announced over the intercom, "Ladies and Gentlemen: I have some bad news and some good news. The bad news is we don't know where we're going. The good news is we're making excellent time!" The choleric may be making record progress boosted by fear of failure, but the end result may be disaster as he surveys those hurt along the way.

The phlegmatic temperament is the quiet, calm, well-organized diplomat with the gracious spirit. These people are often unmotivated and self-righteous. The phlegmatic person rolls with the flow, with the carefree attitude of "Isn't life wonderful." Fear may keep this temperament completely immobilized. The natural pattern here is to get around to it later, so what's the hurry? He may fear stepping out in any direction and a lack of motivation supports this lack of purpose.

All of us can probably recognize ourselves and people we know who exemplify these temperaments. Even my children recognize them, though they don't know the names of each temperament. I walked by the television one day while they happened to be watching a Winnie-the-Pooh movie. After a few minutes of watching with them I said, "You know, within our family we have these Winnie-the-Pooh characters." Before I could elaborate, my children identified which one of us is a melancholy—Eeyore, sanguine—Tigger, and so forth.

Tim LaHaye has developed a temperament analysis test that categorizes the four basic types of temperaments. Through temperament analysis, you can understand the strengths and weaknesses of your personality type and thereby understand how you react naturally to the joys and stresses of life.

While learning about temperaments, God showed me something important. The biggest obstacle I will ever have to overcome in life is myself. As a naturally negative melancholy temperament, I had to learn how to be a positive person. From childhood, I looked at a glass as half empty. My sanguine husband is exactly the opposite, as is my daughter. They look at a glass as half full. Their temperaments make it easier for them to be positive, whereas I had to learn how. I can assure you it's much easier to receive deliverance from fear if you're born with a positive personality.

Praise God, I've been a good student! The exciting thing about identifying your personality temperament is that when you know your weaknesses you can ask the Holy Spirit to help you overcome them. I have realized that I'm not stuck with my negative weakness. Instead of saying, "I can't," I have changed to, "Well, maybe I can, with God's help."

Whether our inborn temperaments are positive or negative, we all need to defeat fear. Otherwise, as adults we can repeat childhood patterns and pass our *own* fears on to our children. The woman who cleans my house is terrified of lightning. Her grandmother made the family turn off all the lights and sit on the sofa in the middle of the room during the slightest thunderstorm. Today, the childhood pattern repeats itself every time she hears the rumble of thunder. Lestine becomes nervous. She wants to go home, turn out the lights and sit on the sofa with her family.

False Peace

Just as Jesus changes our feelings of fear and gives us peace, Satan will try to duplicate that peace. His counterfeit peace only masks our fears.

The daughter of a friend of ours had some very frightening experiences while dating. In high school, she dated a boy of great physical strength who also had a violent temper. As teenagers might view it, they were the perfect couple, the football star and the homecoming queen. Eventually, they attended the same college.

On several occasions, displaying his anger, he would prevent her from leaving her college dormitory. Once she was riding in the car with him when he began driving recklessly, refusing to stop the car and let her out. Eventually she feared for her life when she was with him and she severed this treacherous relationship. Her parents came to college to get her and her belongings, and she transferred to another school closer to home.

The girl's frightening experiences with one young man made her afraid of close relationships with other men. For several years, she kept her relationships with men on a platonic basis. Then she met a young man to whom she drew closer and closer. He loved God, and it seemed as if this might be God's mate for her.

But one day she told me, "I have broken off with my boyfriend, and God has given me a wonderful peace about doing it. Our relationship was getting serious, and that's not what the Lord desires for us."

I felt compelled to ask a few questions. "Leslie, you have had a relationship that brought so much fear in your life. Do you suppose it's possible that your peace isn't true and of God? Could you have a wound based on the fear of commitment to a relationship with a man? Might you be so afraid to trust a man and to be vulnerable emotionally that you just want to run away from commitment?"

My questions made Leslie stop and think. "I don't know," she said. "I never thought about it in those terms."

"You may think you know God's plan for your life, but let's pray and ask Him if your fear was the real reason for your breaking up. He will reveal it to you," I advised her.

I knew Leslie's love for God and her earnest desire to follow Him, so I had no doubt that He would show her whatever she needed to know about this situation—whether she was experiencing real peace or false peace. As she prayed about it, something amazing happened. Every book, every magazine—no matter what she read—mentioned relationships based on fear. Every place she looked, she saw the topic.

One Sunday night about this time, Leslie came to church to hear that the pastor had been called away unexpectedly. A guest speaker had been selected on the spur of the moment without much time to prepare, and he announced, "I believe that tonight God wants to heal damaged relationships that are based on fear."

Leslie sat there stunned.

He then asked for people to come forward for prayer and she was the first one at the altar. God revealed and healed her fear. The young man who loved God and loved her had just recently told the Lord, "You know how much I love her and You know how much I love You. Most of all, I desire You, Lord. If I have to give her up, if she's never to be mine, I give her back to You."

After the service, she found her boyfriend and told him how God had revealed and healed her fear of a relationship with a man. They were reunited, and, a few months later, I watched Leslie in her wedding dress walk down the aisle of the church. The beauty of the moment was enough to bring tears to the eye. But I shed tears of amazement, overwhelmed at the thought of what almost hadn't been.

Sometimes we need others to help us discover the wounds we have hidden and can't even see ourselves. That's the value in the body of Christ, that we strengthen and encourage one another. But it takes both sides. Had it not been for Leslie's willingness to be open and vulnerable, she might have missed God's best for her life. It took strength to look inside and face her fear. Had she not been transparent, my prodding questions might have met firm resistance. But God opened up Leslie's hurt and released the fear.

Fear can grip us and keep us from fulfilling God's plan for our lives. Do you see how Satan was so good at counterfeiting peace to mask fear? But false peace can't stand against the revealing power of the Holy Spirit. When we sincerely ask God to reveal Himself and show us the truth, He does! Then with His light and our willingness we can walk into wholeness if there are wounds to be healed. Once again, God proved Himself the healer of emotions. Real peace, however, sustains this inner prodding and brings lasting contentment in God's direction.

The psalmist puts it this way, "I sought the Lord and he heard me, and delivered me from all my fears" (Ps. 34:4). Talk to God about your fears and seek His deliverance from them.

Assignment for Living

1. Read these scriptures as they relate to fear: 2 Corinthians 10:5; Psalms 34:4; 46:1-2; 56:3-4; 4:8; 1 Timothy 1:7; 1 John 4:18; Joshua 1:9.
2. Ask God to show you, and ask yourself:
   a. What are my fears?
   b. Are they rational or irrational?
   c. How does my temperament influence fear in my life?
   d. Am I a positive person?
   e. Am I as an adult repeating a childhood pattern of fear?
   f. Is there false peace masking a wounded place in my life?
   g. What tangible steps toward conquering fear can I take?
3. As you sincerely ask God to reveal these things to you, allow Him to shine His light into that hurting, fearful place. Allow Him to replace fear with real peace. Give Him time.
4. Pray: Dear Lord, Thank You that You never leave me hanging. You are the perfect answer to all my fears. I ask that You would reveal Yourself to me. Show me where I am afraid. Show me why I'm afraid. Heal those fearful places with Your perfect peace, and give me strength to walk into Your light. I choose to trust You when I am afraid. You are my strength. I love You, Jesus. Amen.

PART III

HEALING THE WOUNDS

TEN

The Road To Wholeness

*I*n the previous chapters, we've identified different kinds of wounds that prevent wholeness—anger, resentment, insecurity, guilt, anxiety, pride and fear. We've learned the importance of discovering those hurting places and admitting them to ourselves and God. But exactly how does Jesus break down the barriers that mask the pain? How does He bring wholeness to these areas of our lives? We have to get past the walls, start becoming transparent, see the wounded places and understand who we really are inside.

Sometimes He heals wounded and damaged emotions with a miracle. The Bible contains many stories of Jesus making people completely whole in an instant.

Have you ever watched an old building being demolished? On television you've probably seen walls collapsing the moment strategically placed explosives are detonated. God can break down a barrier we've built around our pain in just the same way today. Pride, resentment, anger and other long-held feelings can come crashing down, crumbling into nothingness.

Slowly but Surely

But God may also bring wholeness gradually. God loves us enough to work with us step by step, leading us in the right path toward wholeness.

When we were remodeling our house, an exterior brick wall needed to come down. We had to chisel out the mortar around each brick and tear down the wall one brick at a time. God often works that way in our lives. The barriers of our lives come down brick by single brick. As the wall comes down, more of His light shines through. No barrier blocks its transmission.

I believe God is doing this for my brother. Two years ago, he went through a difficult time in his life. I remember praying, "God, bring him to a place where he sees his need for You." The Holy Spirit spoke to my burdened heart telling me to bind a spirit of spiritual rejection on his behalf. I remember thinking, *What is that? I've never heard of such a thing.*

For a year and a half I prayed for him, even though I didn't understand why I was supposed to bind a spirit of spiritual rejection. Last year, I had a conversation with my brother and asked him, "What happened to cause you to walk away from God?"

He told me, "Carolyn, when the kids in my

church got turned on for God, the church considered us a threat and dispersed us. The kids at school called me a Jesus freak. I couldn't stand the pressure so I started doing things the other kids would accept. I knew God wouldn't forgive me for my past, so I blew Him off."

The sound of these words screamed in my ear. There was that spirit of spiritual rejection. My brother believed the lie that God wouldn't forgive him. Those words, "I knew God wouldn't forgive me," reverberated over and over in my mind. I knew why God had me pray specifically against the spirit of spiritual rejection.

Now my brother is on the road to rebuilding his life, knowing God forgives him and loves him.

Many of us tear down walls only halfway. We feel His light penetrate an area of our lives, and then we stop the breaking-down process.

After that initial feeling of relief, we settle for a little bit of victory. We may be pleased with a partial healing. We may not realize how wounded we still are. We may think, *Oh good. It's gone. I won't ever have to deal with that again.*

Later we discover the wounds were not completely healed. Satan will protest, "See, it didn't go away after all. You still have that same ugly old problem. You're not going to make it."

Satan makes us feel guilty when an emotion or feeling crops up again. Let's say, for example, that you think you have resolved anger. Then something happens and anger returns. The enemy will scoff, "You never dealt with your anger. See, it's still part of you."

But it takes a long time to change a pattern you have lived since childhood. When Satan tries to make you feel guilty while God is helping you knock down a barrier, stand on 2 Corinthians 10:5, which says you are to cast down imaginations and bring every thought into the obedience of Christ. Refuse to listen to the enemy and don't accept guilt when you know God is breaking down the barrier.

God wants to remove these barriers completely. Remember that tearing down a wall, brick by brick, takes time. It's a slow process we sometimes don't understand. Let me compare this emotional process to physical healing. A scab will form on top of a severe cut. After a period of time, a child tends to pick at the scab, pulling it off to look at the wound. Surprisingly, it still looks ugly and inflamed. But it has been healing, a little at a time.

Similarly, we can't see the entire healing process taking place within us. On the surface, a barrier may appear to be gone, when the healing is continuing underneath.

In Colossians 3 the apostle Paul tells us to mortify our members or put to death certain parts of ourselves, and to "put on the new man, which is renewed in knowledge after the image of him that created him" (vv. 5,9,10).

The Fruit of the Spirit

Paul was writing about our role in the breaking down or healing process. The old person puts off anger, resentment, guilt and pride to become a new person with Christlike characteristics. To do this, we must be willing to let God reign on the throne of our lives. As we allow God that first position, He replaces the wounds with the fruit of the Spirit, which are the characteristics of Christ.

The fruit are the evidence that God is maturing us spiritually. Hebrews 6:1 in the Living Bible says it so plainly, "Let us stop going over the same old ground again and again, always teaching those first lessons about Christ. Let us go on instead to other things and become mature in our understanding, as strong Christians ought to be." To become mature in our understanding, we need to look inside at those wounds that keep us in bondage, that block this road to wholeness. Paul writes in Galatians 5:1, "Stand fast therefore in the liberty wherewith Christ hath made us free, and be not entangled again with the yoke of bondage."

Wounds of anxiety, fear, pride, guilt or rejection are yokes of bondage. Have you ever seen yoked oxen? They are bound together, plowing the same ground, row after row, day after day. In the same way wounds are not healed, and as the ruts get deeper, the wound gets deeper and we're stuck in bondage to these yokes until Jesus brings freedom. Oxen are known as beasts of burden. Similarly, the yokes of bondage burden you down and hinder you from enjoying wholeness. Many times people think they're stuck with the yokes. Have you ever heard someone say, "I'm just a fearful person," accepting the notion that nothing can be changed. Or "I have such a temper. Our family has always been full of screamers." The implication is that that's just the way it is.

God never intended us to live in bondage to this kind of yoke. Paul admonishes us to stand in the liberty of Christ and not be entangled with the yoke of bondage. And how do we get out from under the yokes? By allowing God to develop the fruit of the Spirit in our lives!

In Galatians 5:22,23, Paul lists the fruit of the Spirit—love, joy, peace, long-suffering, gentleness, goodness, meekness, temperance and faith. This fruit provides the evidence that God is breaking down our barriers and changing our feelings. You'll know He has broken down the barrier of anxiety when the fruit of peace grows up in its place. Faith will abide in place of fear. Meekness will blossom instead of pride.

When John and I were newlyweds, I found myself short on temperance. One night while we were eating dinner, I was telling him about a problem I was having with another person. John remarked, "Carolyn, the trouble with you is that you don't have any backbone."

I had just picked up a bite of potato salad on my fork and somehow, with no thought and one small flick of the wrist, that potato salad mysteriously hit John's cheek. Both of us broke into gales of laughter and chuckled through the rest of the meal. He's never said that to me again. But if he did, I hope I would have the temperance to hold on to my potato salad.

Another fruit of the Spirit that God wants to develop in us is joy. Joy should be like a deep, flowing current within us, no matter what the circumstances. Happiness differs from joy in that happiness is tied to the conditions around us.

Before we built our home, when we were planning for construction, we hit a snag and thought we wouldn't be able to build. The delays and difficulties made me very unhappy and disappointed. But in spite of the surface emotions, I felt a deep joy within that never went away, knowing God was in control of our lives. It was exciting to me to identify the difference between happiness and joy and to experience the joy that runs deep and comes from God.

If we're walking closely with the Father, He uses one particular fruit of the Spirit, peace, as an indication of His will. I was invited to a certain function that I felt I should attend. Actually, I wanted to go, but I also felt the Lord nudging me not to. *I really ought to go. It's the nice, polite thing to do. It's the socially acceptable thing to do,* I reasoned with Him. But every time I seriously considered going, I'd be filled with anxiety. In His love for me, God went further and revealed to me through His Word why I wasn't supposed to attend this function. Peace returned when I finally decided I would not go. It was a heart-rending time of communicating with God. When I put away my personal desire to attend this function, the anxiety lifted and peace returned.

He taught me another important lesson about peace when I was battling fear. Often I'd quote Isaiah 26:3, "Thou wilt keep him in perfect peace, whose mind is stayed on thee." One day I opened my Bible and read the verse in its entirety. I found I'd missed the complete message of the Scripture.

It actually reads, "Thou wilt keep him in perfect peace, whose mind is stayed on thee: *because* he trusteth in thee" (italics mine).

I discovered the key to peace. I'd thought the verse meant, "God, You will keep me in perfect peace if my mind is stayed on You." In reality, the reason I am kept in perfect peace as I meditate on Christ is because I trust Him enough to let Him into my life.

Faith is another fruit that the Lord grows as we surrender ourselves to Him.

Second Chronicles 16:9 says, "For the eyes of the Lord run to and fro throughout the whole earth, to shew himself strong in the behalf of them whose heart is perfect toward him." The psalmist writes, "Thou knowest my downsitting and mine uprising, thou understandest my thought afar off. Thou compassest my path and my lying down, and art acquainted with all my ways" (Ps. 139:2,3).

Do these verses speak of a detached God who has little interest in our lives? On the contrary, they tell us how much He cares for us. His concern for us is like that of a mother's for her children. What mother's heart doesn't go out to her children, especially when they confront problems. A daughter knows her mother cares what happens to her. A son trusts his mother to take care of him no matter what the circumstances. In just the same way, we trust God because we know He cares about us.

One of my sons went through a tough situation in school that taught me a lesson about faith. As

I was praying for God to solve the situation, He spoke to me about Shadrach, Meshach and Abednego in the Book of Daniel. I responded by saying, "Thank You, Lord, for reminding me that You delivered them out of the fiery furnace. I believe You've delivered my son out of this situation at school." With faith I concluded my prayer.

But when I went to pick up the children at school that afternoon, the situation had gone from bad to worse. In the car driving home, I told God honestly, "I don't understand. You reminded me about the three Hebrew men whom You delivered out of the fiery furnace. Why didn't You deliver my son out of this situation?"

God let me know I needed to read that Bible story again and see what had happened before He delivered them out of the fire. Nebuchadnezzar warned the three that they had no chance of survival in the furnace. The men responded by stating their trust in God. They said God was able to deliver them out of the fire, *but even if He did not,* they would still believe that He was almighty Jehovah God (see Dan. 3:17-19).

God gave me a new insight into this familiar story. I learned the importance of faith—whether or not He delivers me from my fiery trial. He taught me that we are to trust Him because He is almighty God, not just because of what we want Him to do for us. God is in control, no matter what the circumstances. When I trusted Him implicitly, He delivered my son, solving the problem at school.

Not long afterwards, a good friend of mine

phoned me. "I'll be checking into the hospital soon," Carol started. Her voice broke, reflecting her concern. "I've got a numbness in my arm. The doctors are sure it's caused by either multiple sclerosis or a brain tumor."

When I hung up the telephone, I prayed for her. God took me back to that same Scripture passage of the three men in the fire. He gave me still another insight into their story. As I reread the account, I came to the place in Daniel 3:25 where the king said, "I see four men loose, walking in the midst of the fire and they have no hurt; and the form of the fourth is like the Son of God." God's revelation hit me. The three men did not come *out* of the fire *until* they had walked *in* the fire with Jesus. God took their one seed of faith and made it grow into ripe fruit.

I called Carol back. "God has spoken to me through His Word while I was praying for you. He is going to deliver you out of this, but you must trust Him no matter what happens." I shared with her how the three men walked through the fire with Jesus before He delivered them. Incredibly, she had just been reading the same passage of the Bible. We realized that God was speaking supernaturally to us.

She determined to walk through the situation, even though the prognosis pointed to sober conclusions. In the hospital, the doctors ran all sorts of tests and didn't find multiple sclerosis or a brain tumor. She eventually entered the Mayo Clinic where, again, all tests were negative. Carol put herself in God's hands and He brought her through the furnace of affliction (see Is. 48:10). It wasn't easy, but God was faithful. He healed her.

The Bible describes David as a man after God's own heart (see Acts 13:22). He displayed faith in spite of circumstances. One thing I love about David is that he was honest with himself and God. Many of his psalms detail despair and complaint: "God, where have You gone? What's happened to me?"

"Woe is me," he would wail. In Psalm 102 he pours out his complaint to God: "Hide not thy face from me in the day when I am in trouble....For my days are consumed like smoke, and my bones are burned as the hearth. My heart is smitten and withered like grass: so that I forget to eat my bread....I am like a pelican of the wilderness: I am like an owl of the desert" (vv. 2,3,4,6). And yet in the end his faith was in God. Our church sings David's words, "Be exalted, O God, above the heavens: let thy glory be over all the earth" (Ps. 108:5). David wrote that while hiding in a cave, thinking Saul was going to kill him at any moment.

Another verse we sing says, "Thy lovingkindness is better than life, my lips shall praise thee. Thus will I bless thee while I live" (Ps. 63:3,4). David penned these words while running for his life in the desert. Once again, Saul was pursuing him, yet in his distress, David's faith was renewed. Life wasn't easy, and David admitted that to God, but as he did so, he looked to Him repeatedly for His strength.

Job, in his destruction, disease and despair,

expressed complete faith in the Lord. "Though he slay me, yet will I trust in him" (Job 13:15). Again we see his humanity in his complaint, yet the bottom line is that God increased Job's faith.

The Gifts of the Spirit

God uses not only the fruit of the Spirit to replace our wounds, but He also uses the gifts of the Spirit, which are named in 1 Corinthians 12: the word of wisdom, word of knowledge, faith, healing, working of miracles, prophecy, discerning of spirits, tongues and interpretation of tongues.

What do these gifts do? For one thing, they show us how much God cares about us. He cares enough to speak specifically through a supernatural utterance and give supernatural power for a particular need. Through the gifts of the Spirit, we receive a greater revelation of God. It's another avenue to a closer relationship with Him as God in His omnipotence communicates His truth through His supernatural power. While the fruit of the Spirit are the replacement for wounds that develop on our walk to wholeness, the gifts of empowerment come through God's grace as He leads and guides us as we walk in the Spirit.

God used a gift of the Spirit when John and I were helping someone through his difficulties. We had prayed and counseled, done everything we knew to do with no apparent progress. The person's situation had not improved.

I prayed in despair, "God, what's going to happen? This situation is getting worse and we don't have any answers. We don't know what else to do, and time is running out.''

As I cried out to God He gave me a message through the gift of prophecy. Words formed so fast I raced for a pencil and paper. As I wrote the words, I quickly realized they were not from me. In fact, the words were unlike me.

Just as I had finished writing two pages, the urgency to write turned to calmness. When I read what I had written, I was overwhelmed by the tremendous compassion in this message. God's words to the person going through the difficult days spoke of His love and care and said that He would soon provide the answer to the situation.

Tears flowed freely as the person read the message God had given through me. And three weeks later, the answer came. It amazed me how God, in His perfect timing, knew exactly what this person needed and gave a prophecy to give him courage to hold on a little longer.

God also uses the gift of knowledge to work in our lives. Here's an illustration of that gift in action. John and I were asked to speak at a church. He was scheduled to speak in the worship service, and I was asked to speak to the adult Sunday school classes.

John accompanied me to the combined classes where I shared what God wanted me to say. Nearing the end of the class session, I sensed the Holy Spirit telling me emphatically to quit and sit down.

But there are two more points I wanted to make, I reminded Him. The Holy Spirit instructed me again clearly to stop speaking. So I closed my Bible, told the class, ''Thank you very much,'' and sat down.

It was such an abrupt ending that it caught the pastor, sitting on the front row, off guard. He quickly stood up. "John, would you like to say a few words?" he asked. "We still have a little time."

John has no trouble with impromptu speaking. He can always think of something to talk about. If I were asked to speak extemporaneously, I'd think, *Oh my, what am I going to say?* But John gladly spoke for the remaining five minutes or so of class time.

After the worship service, at least fifteen people approached us with comments like, "John, what you said in those five minutes was exactly why God had me come today. I needed to hear that."

God imparted the gift of knowledge for that particular occasion. You see, God already knows our hearts, and He knows our needs, so He reaches out to us through the gifts of the Spirit. He moves through the gifts on our behalf to bring us to the place we need to be. Hearing the confirming remarks of those people made me grateful I had listened and sat down!

Let me relate a personal experience in which God moved by giving another gift of the Spirit, discernment.

While our house was under construction, I kept feeling unrest about an electrician who was installing the wiring. For some unknown reason, this man's presence troubled me. Finally, I talked to the builder who was a Christian. "I don't know why," I said, "but something bothers me about this electrician. I know God is speaking to me, but I don't know what the problem is."

The builder believed God had a reason for speaking to me about this man. So he questioned the electrician's partner. "I want to know what's going on here. What's the problem with Charlie?"

"How did you know?" his partner replied.

"I just know there's a problem and I want to know what it is," the builder persisted.

"Well...the man's an alcoholic," his partner answered.

God knew the situation and cared enough to reveal it to us. He extended His love to a man caught in bondage, which led to improved communication between the partners. When Charlie understood how much the people around him cared, he admitted his need for help and eventually went to Alcoholics Anonymous.

When I was fighting fear, God gave me the gift of faith, which differs from the fruit of faith in that the gift comes supernaturally for a particular need.

Several years ago, I heard the testimony of a man named Mel Tari, the author of *Like a Mighty Wind*. His testimony, like his book, told of a great revival in Indonesia.

Tari said the Indonesians received the Word of God, believing it in its entirety. They'd never heard theologians debating whether some scriptures were right or wrong. He went on to tell about the dramatic, miraculous events that occurred as he was traveling from village to village. As Tari was walking through the underdeveloped land, he and his companions came upon a lion who looked none too friendly. Tari had read in Genesis 1:28 where God had given men dominion over "every living thing that creepeth over the earth." No one in the group had any weapons, so in the name of Jesus they commanded the lion to leave. And it turned around and walked away!

As I sat listening to Tari, I thought, *What a wonderful testimony.* My faith was increased, and God knew ahead of time why I needed to hear this story. The very next day while I was talking on the telephone, I heard some noise coming from my bedroom. Stretching the cord and looking down the hall, I saw my then two-year-old son, Randy. He was barefoot and kicking at a poisonous coral snake on the carpet! Our miniature dachshund stood by, barking his head off.

I was extremely fearful of snakes. Knowing that, God gave me a supernatural gift of faith. With absolutely no fear, I walked in the bedroom. I took Randy and the dog to the far end of the house. Then I walked back to the kitchen, got a butcher knife out of the drawer and headed back to the bedroom. Staring down at the snake, I rebuked it boldly, "In the name of Jesus, you have no authority in my home. Put your head down and hold still."

The viper did so, and I cut his head off. It took awhile, too, because my butcher knife was dull. I placed the corpse in a sack, carried it out to the garage and collapsed!

I'm glad I collapsed. God knew I didn't need to walk around saying, "Look what I did." He had

given me His supernatural gift of faith at that particular time for fighting my fear of snakes.

The fruit of the Spirit and the gifts of the Spirit
enable us to walk away from the wounds that have
beset us for so long. Only in God will we find
wholeness.

ELEVEN

Lord, What's My Next Step?

While John and I were traveling in North Carolina, we planned a shopping trip to a nearby factory outlet store. I hate these places, but John loves a bargain. Racks of clothing filled the huge warehouse structure. Wheeling a grocery cart to carry our purchases, we set out in search of the men's suits.

Soon we found the rack for John's size. It seemed to stretch as far as we could see. We finally selected a couple of suits and made our way across the building to the dressing rooms. The area was crowded so I waited outside while he tried on the suits. He found a salesclerk who handed him a little, plastic coat hanger with the number "6" printed on it. Of course this meant he had six pieces of clothing.

But John, who hates to shop anyway, didn't

know what the number represented. He pushed the cart of suits into the dressing room, looked at the "6" and surveyed the dressing room doors. The factory outlet had only one section of dressing rooms which were used by both men and women. As you'd expect, the doors were not numbered, but John was sure he understood the system and he counted—one, two, three, four, five, six—and opened the door.

A woman screamed, and John shut the door immediately, muttering profuse apologies. He came out of the dressing room entrance looking terribly bewildered. He handed the salesclerk the number and explained, "Um, somebody's in that one."

With a condescending look, the salesclerk said, "That's the number of pieces of clothing you have, sir."

Standing out of hearing range, I wondered what was happening to John. He certainly had not been in the dressing room long enough to have tried on the suits. Later, much later, we both had a good laugh about his embarrassing moment. His humorous experience emphasizes the need for clear directions. Without proper guidance, we muddle through life in a daze.

God wants to direct us, but we must choose to follow His direction; we must choose to be in relationship with Him.

Psalm 32:8 says, "I will instruct thee and teach thee in the way which thou shalt go: I will guide thee with mine eye." I dislike the next verse because I identify with it. "Be ye not as a horse, or the mule, which have no understanding: whose mouth must be held in with bit and bridle, lest they come near unto thee."

I'm just chicken-hearted enough to want the easy way. I want to be guided by His eye—the way a child knows whether the look in his mother's eye means "be still" or "be careful." But Jesus' guidance isn't quite that simple. He wants us to tune in to His plan for our lives; He never constrains us roughly to follow His way. He did not make us as pawns on a chessboard or puppets on a string.

One time I was pouring my counseling frustrations out to God in prayer. (Often the people who come to me for counseling are not dedicated believers.)

I said, "Lord, I know that what these people need is You. I know they need to read Your Word. They need to find out who You are. I know that's their answer. But all they want from me is a Band-Aid. They want a quick fix for their problems because they are hurting. I don't know what to do."

Instead of addressing the problem I saw, God confronted *me*. He pointed out that I was just like my counselees. He said He had taught me some things but had much more to teach me. God let me know that if I didn't listen to Him, spend time with Him and really open myself to Him, He couldn't teach me either.

The Bible says, "Choose you this day whom ye will serve" (Josh. 24:15). "I have set before you life and death, blessing and cursing: therefore choose life" (Deut. 30:19). God gave us a free will to make the choice. We can choose to say, "God, I'm going to let You into my life. I'm going to let You reveal those wounds that I don't want to look at." Otherwise, we choose the opposite and live fragmented lives, never acknowledging our pain or need of God.

Psychologists say there is tremendous power in the word "choose." When Andrew's first grade teacher was disciplining him, she gave him sentences to write. I chuckled when he brought his paper home. Ten times he had written, "I choose to," and he had left off the word the teacher had then pencilled in red—"obey." He wasn't sure what he had written, but he had chosen it ten times.

If we choose to let God in, He will direct us, but we must learn to listen to Him. The open communication He desires with us should be two-way. He listens to us as we talk to Him, and we listen to Him as He talks to us.

While we need childlike trust, our prayers shouldn't sound childish. Too often we communicate with God like little children who run to Father calling, "Daddy, Daddy, listen to everything I want." We pray, "Lord, I need this, bless so and so and take care of me. Thank You, Lord. Amen." Before God can speak to *us*, we're off and running. We've deposited our requests, as we do our money at a bank drive-in teller window, and we're gone.

But God, the Wisdom of the ages, often reveals Himself—and thereby the wounds that keep us from being whole before Him—slowly. In Isaiah

55:8,9 we read that His ways are not our ways.

Our pastor, Alex Clattenburg, has taught us the importance of waiting on God. I've tried to incorporate into my life the lessons Alex has learned. Waiting on God means telling Him, "Here I am, Lord. I just want You to know I am available. Tell me what You want me to do."

In a time when I needed encouragement God spoke so specifically through His Word, that I marveled at how clearly it detailed my life. I was seeking Him regarding direction for what He had called me to do. Doors weren't opening, and in my impatience I questioned. "Did I really hear Your voice? Was I really supposed to go in this direction?"

I had thought He was directing me to help hurting Christians identify wounds so God can heal. While I have a burden for the unsaved I usually focus on Christians who have never been healed from emotional pain. As I opened the Word, I turned to Philippians 4:3: "Yes, I ask you, loyal yokefellow, help these women who have contended at my side in the cause of the gospel... whose names are in the book of life" (NIV).

I sat there stunned. The word "yokefellow" had special meaning to me because God used a yokefellow group in our lives to begin this look inside—to discover who I really was! Now, in addition, His Word assured me that I was to help believers. After those words, I felt I could wait forever for the doors to open. And because God's timing is perfect, the doors opened on His schedule. But how generous of my Father to encourage me. How great His love!

Bob Mumford, in his book *Take Another Look at Guidance*, mentions that there are three harbor lights in the English Channel. The jagged cliffs are so dangerous that the captain of a ship must keep all three lights lined up and in focus to avoid a wreck.

Similarly, three light beams or channels of divine guidance must "line up" to keep us from "ship wrecking" our lives. Moment after moment we are faced with decisions that lead us toward wholeness or away from it, and with each decision we should consider the three channels of guidance.

God's Word

The first one is God's Word. Is what you're doing consistent with the Word of God? If it's not, you already know it's not right and it will lead you away from wholeness. You don't have to look any further.

John and I were counseling someone with marital problems when the person remarked, "Well, maybe it was never God's will for me to marry my spouse in the first place, so maybe I should get a divorce."

"Wait a minute, "I insisted. "Let's see what God says about this." The three of us searched God's Word and found that divorce was not the right direction for this marriage.

One day while I was praying, I asked God specifically, "Show me whether or not I'm on the right path for my life. And if I'm not, Lord, show me the right path." Afterward, I opened my Bible to the chapters which I'd been reading. On the page I turned to, one passage was underlined in red. The verse said, "His God instructs him and teaches him the right way" (Is. 28:26). Through His Word, God assured me specifically that He would show me because I asked Him.

When I was fighting my fear of fire, God spoke to me about a particular passage in Romans. I replied, "Lord, I already know what Romans 8 says. It doesn't have anything to do with deliverance from my fear of fire."

I'm thankful that God, the Creator of the universe, condescends into our everyday lives to have relationship with us. We can trust Him to talk to us and we can talk back to Him. I'm not proud of the fact that I sometimes retort to an omnipotent God, but I know He's not going to kick me out of the kingdom for it. His love transcends, enabling me to communicate with Him as I would communicate with you.

Obediently, I picked up a Bible, a paraphrased edition which I don't usually read. Turning to Romans, I glanced above chapter 8 and saw a verse I'd underlined in the previous chapter. Those words, the only ones underlined on the page, spoke directly to me concerning my need of deliverance from fear. "There is something else deep within me, in my lower nature, that is at war with my mind and wins the fight and makes me a slave to the sin that is still within me" (Rom. 7:23, TLB).

"Thank You, Lord," I cried from the depths of my heart. I realized I couldn't fight the war against fear alone. I needed someone to pray for me and in the name of Jesus command the fear of fire to leave me. And God delivered me from that fear.

How do we learn what God's Word says? By reading it. One way to get to know someone is by reading what they wrote. It doesn't happen overnight, but eventually the words of Scripture flow through your mind.

It takes work to get into and know the Scripture. It takes work to memorize the Word so God's guidance is at your fingertips when you need it most.

Let's say that fear keeps returning to your thoughts. Memorizing the Word will help heal that wound. It's like a soothing ointment. But be sure you understand what you memorize. I remember picking up Andrew after a Royal Ranger meeting. The church organization for young boys requires them to memorize verses as part of their advancement program.

Another mother had arrived to pick up her son, and I overheard their conversation. She was obviously frustrated because her son had not quoted John 3:16 for his commander. Even though she took him to the corner of the room to talk, she protested loudly, "Johnny, you know John 3:16. I taught it to you. Now I want you to say it."

The little boy, wearing a blank expression on his face, looked up at his mother. She said, "Go ahead, Johnny, right now—say John 3:16. 'Do unto others as you would have them do unto you.' " I thought, *Oh, I hope I can get out of this room before I burst out laughing.* I hoped she found out soon that she'd quoted the Golden Rule.

I've found it easy to memorize Scripture verses when I sing them. Our church teaches many songs straight from the Word, and I find these songs running through my mind as I go about my daily tasks. I've often made up tunes to Scripture myself. It makes learning it easier for me.

The Holy Spirit

God gives direction not only through His Word, but also through a second channel of guidance—the leading and speaking of the Holy Spirit. When seeking direction, ask yourself, "How is the Holy Spirit leading me?"

As I was seeking God about prayer for deliverance in my life, I sensed the Holy Spirit's leading through a particular instance. While watering my plants one day, I accidentally knocked a pot over, spilling a little dirt on the carpet. Such a small amount of dirt didn't warrant dragging out the vacuum cleaner. So I did what any good homemaker does to hide dirt, I spread it around, allowing the carpet fibers to cover the soil!

As I was scattering the dirt down into the carpet, the Holy Spirit spoke to me saying, "That's just like your life. No matter how little the dirt in your life, no matter how well it's hidden, it's still within you and you don't need it." When I understood, I couldn't get to someone fast enough to pray for me. Why would I want to hold onto anything that wasn't from God?

When we meditate upon, listen to and wait on God, He will tell us what we need to know through His Word and by His Spirit. By following these channels of divine guidance, God will break down the barriers in our lives and, in turn, in the lives of other people.

A television talk show, broadcast live on a local station, scheduled a program on the subject of adoption. As the mother of three adopted children, I was asked to appear on this program.

The thought of speaking on television made me nervous and frightened, so I started praying about what to say. Sitting at my kitchen table a few hours before the program, I suddenly felt God's peace replace my fear. He assured me that from that moment on I would never be afraid to speak on adoption. He told me at the beginning of the program to speak these specific words: "For some people, adoption is not God's alternative. It's His first choice."

I obeyed and every call from the viewers during the program centered on that first comment. God moved by His Spirit because He knew what the people needed to hear.

The Holy Spirit moved through John and me on another occasion to break down the barriers of unforgiveness in others. We were invited to speak to a group of people in a nearby city, and we spent the days before the engagement praying about what God wanted us to share. One day John came home for lunch and I said, "God has spoken to me about talking on the subject of forgiveness." John had felt God's leading to share on the same subject. Our similar thoughts confirmed to us what God wanted us to say.

Several days later we walked into the gathering

of people we had never met, except for the hostess. We were welcomed warmly by fellow Christians who looked like wonderful people. As I greeted them, I thought, *I'm not supposed to talk to these lovely people about forgiveness.* I got alone in the bathroom and questioned the Lord: "Are You sure we're to talk to these people about forgiveness? They are lovely caring people. They don't need a message about that. I've looked at them, and they're fine."

God heard my question and answered me right there. "You've looked at them through your eyes, right?"

"Right," I responded, and I heard nothing more from Him. I had looked at them through my eyes which see the outer person, but He knows the inner person. God knows what's behind the masks that separate people from each other and Him.

So we went ahead and spoke on forgiveness, and the people responded overwhelmingly. God already knew their hearts and broke the unforgiveness that held them in bondage.

Circumstances

God also guides us through circumstances. He is a God of reason and order, guiding us by His Word, by His Spirit and through circumstances.

I remember reading about a minister who heard God tell him to go to Peru. The man looked at the first two channels and saw that they lined up. First of all, he knew his calling was consistent with God's Word because it fulfilled the great commission. Second, he felt the leading of the Holy Spirit; he knew God had called him to win the lost. As a result, he resigned from a very effective ministry, sold everything he owned, uprooted his family and took them to Peru. But his evangelism efforts failed, and they returned to the United States. He had not sought God for His perfect timing nor been sensitive to circumstances lining up.

Fifteen years later he ministered in Peru, and thousands of people were saved. God spoke to him, explaining the difference in the impact of his ministry. It had to do with waiting for God's timing. He hadn't listened for the clearance of the third harbor light.

This man of God had found direction from two of the harbor lights, but had not waited for the right circumstances.

God used these harbor lights in my life when I was praying for my dad's salvation. Before going to witness to him, God spoke to me from His Word. I was experiencing turmoil because I knew it would be difficult for me to confront Dad about his soul.

The verse God kept repeating to me was 2 Chronicles 20:17, "Stand ye still, and see the salvation of the Lord with you...fear not, nor be dismayed; tomorrow go out against them: for the Lord will be with you." God gave me that verse knowing I was burdened for my dad's salvation and that I was afraid. He was convicting me by His Spirit in the months preceding our visit to talk to Dad. As I got the confirmation of His Word and leading of the Holy Spirit, I waited for the timing.

We planned a trip to the beach near their home that summer and as the time came closer, John suggested I have lunch with Daddy alone. John would keep the kids, and Daddy and I would have time alone to talk. How I needed that word from the Lord promising salvation because twice my dad completely forgot about the lunch date I'd scheduled to talk to him. Then after I arrived at the restaurant, I got sick.

In the restroom, I was praying and the Lord reminded me of the words, "Fear not, nor be dismayed...go out against them: for the Lord will be with you." I realized my getting sick was a trick of Satan, but the Lord promised to be with me. God's timing was perfect. As Daddy forgot each luncheon date, I grew more determined to witness to him. God knew I would have backed out before, but by the time I'd tried three lunches and fought sickness, I was determined not to give up. As it says in Isaiah 50:7, "I have set my face like flint to do His will" (TLB). After more prayer, I returned to our table feeling well and able to witness to my dad.

In our walk of breaking down walls and looking at the wounds in our lives, we need these harbor lights of God's direction. Use God's Word to speak to you specifically about these hurts, listen to the voice of the Holy Spirit as He shows you the origins of pain and be sensitive to His perfect timing as He brings healing to your life. He arranges the circumstances in our lives according to His perfect timing, but we have to pray and be sensitive to what God says so we can understand His direction.

TWELVE

We Need Help From Friends

As we've discussed, God uses many different ways to break down our barriers and bring us into wholeness. He is not limited to any one way. Although God does the revealing and healing, sometimes it's necessary to talk about our feelings and emotions with someone.

We confess to God by admitting a barrier that He has revealed, but we also may need to confess our faults to one another as part of the healing process (see James 5:16).

We need not only a trusting relationship with God, but also with individuals to whom we confess. We need someone to whom we can unburden our souls. More important, we need to know this person will still love us when we've taken off our masks.

Group sharing helps in the healing process to wholeness. We often tend to exaggerate our own guilt and inadequacies. But when we discover that others in our close-knit groups can know all about us and still accept us, we can better accept ourselves.

Nowadays, many of us don't have the extended family living nearby. A generation ago, aunts, uncles, cousins, grandmothers and parents lived in the same town, sometimes in the same house. Since our extended families live so far away, we've lost the close relationships that might come naturally if it weren't for distance. That's why the body of Christ is so important. Our brothers and sisters in Christ fulfill our need for closeness with other people.

I thank God that He has blessed me with a sharing group. Years ago, during a period of fasting and prayer, God brought John together with a group of five other men and He has since knit all these couples together through a monthly fellowship supper with special added times of family get-togethers as well. We have had wonderful beach trips and celebrations at holidays; we've had children grow up and marry, and now grandchildren have been born to our "family."

Our family's relationships with these families have not always been easy, but it's been one of the most wonderful parts of my life. Just as families have disagreements and misunderstandings, so does the family of God. But it's wonderful to have a relationship where you are accepted just as you are—no matter what that person knows about you.

Recently at one of our meetings I had come with some exciting personal news. I waited all evening for just the right moment, hardly able to contain my excitement. Conversation seemed to shift from one pointless issue to another, and my excitement turned to frustration and then anger. Finally as the evening drew to a close, I blurted out, "I've been sitting here all night waiting for an opening to share something really exciting, and we've discussed nothing of any value all evening." The other members of the group sat there in shocked silence. What I deserved at that point were some choice words about my selfishness, self-pity and martyrdom. What I got instead was unconditional acceptance.

"We're sorry, Carolyn," they replied. "Please tell us what's on your heart."

After I shared my news, they then responded with genuine love and excitement, but it was because they chose to look past my fault and focus on my need. Isn't that what the body of Christ is about?

Cecil Osborne notes that group sharing provides insight and growth for participants. He has written some practical guidelines for group sharing.

He sees Jesus as one example. When the adulteress was brought to Him, He didn't condemn her. He knew and knows people's hearts— their motives—and still He doesn't feel a need to judge them. In the Sermon on the Mount He told listeners that they were not to judge either (Matt. 7:1).

Osborne says,

He [Jesus] dealt with the repentant sinner with infinite compassion. He prayed for those who took His life, "Father, forgive them for they know not what they do." Only God could know the countless cross currents of environment, heredity, human will, human frailty, pride, inferiority, anxiety, and stress that have formed in our lives and decisions. Only God can judge. We cannot.

We can, however, come to know ourselves at a much deeper level by developing a ruthless honesty with ourselves, with others, and with God. Out of such honesty in a loving group can come insights which can make us more than we are. More like Christ who accepts us as we are, but longs for us to be more.[1]

Finding a small group or someone you can trust and share with on this deep feeling level is extremely important, and the best sharing groups include people who are humble enough to admit they need help. No one person should "know it all" and tell everyone else how to live. Each member of a sharing group must love each other and pray for each other. When we dare to unmask within the confines of a loving group of people, we find acceptance.

A dear friend of mine once poured out her heart to our committed group of friends. She suffered from diabetes along with two of her children. She expressed her sorrow at the numerous times she had prayed for healing and the many experiences of all three of them standing in prayer lines only to see no change. The pain of judgment from well-meaning believers who had accused her of not having enough faith for healing poured out as she unburdened her soul. We had a choice—to love unconditionally or add to the rejection she already felt. It was a wonderful time of restoration as the group loved and prayed for her. Even the ones who believed healing depended on having enough faith reacted beyond their personal convictions to love and restore a wounded sister.

Osborne quotes one woman as saying, "I've been reasonably sure no one could ever love me if they really knew what I was like inside."[2] But she felt differently when she started sharing with a small group.

You may believe the same thing, and so you wear a mask to hide the you who is still working toward wholeness.

God will use our uniqueness and our circumstances to help break down the barriers in our lives. No matter who you are or what you've been through, He specializes in working all things together for your good and for His glory.

You may be thinking, *If she only knew what I've been through. God could never bring glory out of that.* But I've seen Him change even the worst situations in a person's life.

One of my friends suffered one of the most debasing instances of rape and incest that I have ever heard. For eleven years, she repressed her horrible secret, burying it deep inside. Some parts she even blocked from her conscious memory.

Eventually, her marriage started to fall apart. John and I reached out to this couple in an effort to bring reconciliation to their marriage. We shared with them, counseled them; we brought them to our church. They opened their hearts to a God who had previously meant only rules and regulations to them. Then God began to heal their emotions and restore their marriage. We helped them through the healing process.

Carol then dealt with the pain of the rape she had hidden for so long. Sometimes God heals layer by layer, and as Carol received healing in her marriage, she realized her wounds went much deeper. She trusted in me a little at a time. She had never told anyone this whole sordid story, and she would relate to me only part of the ordeal and stop to see what I would do with it. Would she be rejected? Would she be judged? As I loved her through her account of these painful details, she remembered even the parts she had blocked out. Brick by brick we chiseled away at the terrible hurt. God loved her and brought healing to this terrible wound.

At first, she said, "Well, I can admit these things to you, but I'll never be able to discuss it with my parents."

I'd agree, "All right. We'll just pray and we'll trust God."

In time, she said, "Now I've shared that with my parents, but I'll never be able to tell anyone else."

I responded, "All right. We'll just keep praying and trusting God." But as He brought wholeness to her fragmented life, she shared with others who had similar hurts. And today God is using her to bring healing to them. God, indeed, can turn anything around and use it for His glory, if we trust Him.

There's no situation that is beyond God's ability to heal and redeem. Certainly, after you read this story, you will agree with me.

John and I had adopted two children, and I wanted to adopt a third child. John felt reluctant at first, realizing my insatiable love for children. "Carolyn, I know you. When we adopt a third, you will want a fourth. Then you'll want five and it will never end." I assured him that a third child was all I wanted to adopt.

After much prayer, we knocked on doors, asking doctors and lawyers to contact us if they knew of a baby available for adoption. Then we began a waiting period. Even though the high abortion rate meant there were fewer babies to adopt, we believed God could give us a child.

Everybody we talked to said, "It's difficult to arrange a third adoption when you've already adopted two children. Other couples have their names on lists and are waiting for their first one. Just be happy with what you have."

While we waited, I prayed, "Lord, if it isn't Your plan for us to have another child, please take away my desire." Instead of lessening, the desire intensified. About two weeks before Andrew was born, I told John, "I know there's nothing on the horizon right now, but I feel that God will give us a child soon."

Two weeks later, John walked into the house and declared, "I have something to tell you that's going to change our lives." My first thought was, *Good, he has sold our dead golf cart and he's going to get it out of the garage.*

Instead he said, "We have a son." I was speechless. I set dinner on the table and couldn't eat; I was so excited. Isn't it amazing that you believe God for something and when it happens, you just can't believe it? My children tell the story, "When Mom got Randy, she cried. When she got Julianne, she cried. And when she got Andrew, she couldn't eat."

A doctor from the nearby naval base had called John and said, "I have a baby here in perfect condition. You have five minutes to decide if you want him." John responded immediately, "I'll be right there."

"It seems the natural mother didn't know she was pregnant until she had an eight-pound, four-ounce baby boy," the doctor said. "I have never seen anything like it. This woman is in such excellent condition that she could get up and walk out of here right after giving birth. The mother checked into two hospitals during her pregnancy, saying she was pregnant. Both times she was admitted. They ran complete tests on her, and every test proved negative. The doctors told her she had a thyroid problem. This woman went through military basic training six months pregnant, had no prenatal care and delivered a perfectly healthy baby boy."

John and I were overwhelmed at such a miracle

of God. We thought, *God will go to any lengths to answer prayer, won't He?*

We chose the name Andrew for our son because we liked the name and because the disciple Andrew always brought people to Jesus. A week after we brought Andrew home from the hospital, we received his medical sheet.

Listed on this record was information we would need to know about Andrew. Everything else, such as the mother's name and address, was marked out. However, we found one item in the upper right hand corner of the sheet that had not been marked out. It was a blank labeled Abortions, and she had written the number "1."

God spoke to us saying, "That's the reason his name is Andrew. Like Brother Andrew who smuggled Bibles behind the Iron Curtain, I hid the truth from the doctors and I smuggled him in." We were even more overwhelmed to think that God hid the truth from the medical personnel.

Doctors, bound by an oath, couldn't run all those tests and lie. They couldn't run tests and decide, "We aren't going to tell her she is pregnant because she will abort the baby." That means every test had to have been negative.

So we don't call our son Andy or Drew, we call him Andrew, because we realize that God planned to save his life long ago—to smuggle him in. Yet his birth is no more miraculous than the fact that God wants to save our lives too. He wants to save us from a life of masks and barriers and bring us into complete, total wholeness. By knowing Him and knowing ourselves, we can live transparent before God so that He can shine His light through us, not just to heal us but to use us to heal others.

Satan tries to hinder the process to wholeness by keeping you isolated, thinking no one understands. That shows the importance of group sharing. Everybody's suffering. Everybody's hurting for one reason or another. You've probably heard the familiar quote, "There's strength in numbers." By sharing in a group setting, we can bear one another's burdens (see Gal. 6:2).

Have you ever heard the story behind the song "Tie a Yellow Ribbon 'Round the Old Oak Tree"? It seems there was a young man who rebelled against his father. The young man decided he could not stay at home any longer because his father didn't understand him and he didn't understand his father.

The son left home carrying a lot of hostility and anger within and was gone for many years. His parents never stopped praying and believing for their son, although they never heard anything from him and never knew his whereabouts.

One day a letter arrived in the mail. The mother recognized her son's handwriting. With trembling hands, she opened the envelope. He had written, "Mother, I have done wrong. After being away these many years, I desire to come home. But I don't know how Dad would receive my homecoming. I don't want to make this hard on him, so this is what I'm going to do.

"I'm going to take the train into town. When the train travels past the orchard near the house, I'll look out the window. If it's all right with Dad for me to come home, ask him to tie something white on one of the trees. If I don't see anything white, I'll know he has not forgiven me, then I'll stay on the train. It will be easier for both of us that way."

Finally, the day came when the son boarded the train for home. He was riding down the tracks, getting more and more anxious as the train approached the orchard. He wondered what he would see when he looked out the window. Would his father accept him? Would there be anything white tied to the tree?

What do you think he saw as the orchard came into view? Did he see a piece of cloth? No. He saw sheets and towels and pillowcases and undershirts and blankets. Every white thing the family owned was tied to the tree limbs in the orchard. The father wanted him home!

This story overwhelms me whenever I share it for it depicts God's desire for the body of Christ.

As members of His family, we must love and hold up one another. As a family, we can help one another through the healing process to wholeness and bring one another home.

Afterword

As you read the Word, meditate and ask God to make you whole, I hope you will discover, admit and deal with your emotions. I can't encourage you enough to continue your journey to wholeness. You may feel as though you are being turned inside out. I understand how you feel because I know it hurts to look honestly at yourself. But I can promise you that finding out who you really are is worth every bit of the effort.

Let's pray: Dear God, I thank You that You have called me to wholeness. You said that You would bind up the brokenhearted. I praise You for providing emotional healing. Lord, I pray that You will reveal and heal wounds by shining the light of Your love on every area of my life. Change my feelings and bring me into wholeness, I pray. In Jesus' name, Amen.

Notes

Chapter 1

1. J. Grant Howard, *The Trauma of Transparency* (Portland, Oreg.: Multnomah Press, 1981), pp. 26-27.
2. Charles Swindoll, *Dropping Your Guard* (Waco, Tex.: Word Books, 1983), p. 11.
3. Ibid., p. 9-10.

Chapter 2

1. William J. Gaither, "I Am Loved," 1978.
2. Howard, *The Trauma of Transparency*, p. 70.
3. Twila Paris, "The Warrior Is a Child," 1984.

Chapter 3

1. Cecil Osborne, *The Art of Understanding Yourself* (Grand Rapids, Mich.: Zondervan, 1967), p. 92.
2. Ibid., p. 15.

Chapter 5

1. Osborne, *The Art of Understanding Yourself*, p. 19.

Chapter 6

1. Everett L. Fullam, *Riding the Wind* (Altamonte Springs,

Fla.: Creation House, 1986), p. 92.

Chapter 7

1. Bert Ghezzi, *Transforming Problems* (Ann Arbor, Mich.: Servant Books, 1986), pp. 87-88.
2. Osborne, *The Art of Understanding Yourself*, p. 59.

Chapter 9

1. Tim LaHaye, *LaHaye Temperament Analysis* (El Cajon, Calif.: Family Life Seminars, 1979).

Chapter 12

1. Osborne, *The Art of Understanding Yourself*, p. 158.
2. Ibid., p. 188.

OTHER PUBLICATIONS
OF INTEREST FROM
CREATION HOUSE

The Emerging Christian Woman
by Anne Gimenez

Women are on the move. They are shaking off many years of silence and passivity. Inspired by the Spirit, they are assuming their proper roles of leadership in the body of Christ. Anne believes Christ is calling Christian women to take a lead in bringing new life, healing and unity to the church. $4.95

Spiritual Power and Church Growth
by C. Peter Wagner

Why do some churches grow like wildfire? How can we learn from this marvelously successful church growth movement? C. Peter Wagner identifies the main reasons for the expansion of Pentecostal churches and articulates key principles behind their growth in Latin America. With examples, stories and facts, he writes about how to engage the power of the Holy Spirit; involving new Christians in ministry; cell groups; training leaders in service; the importance of signs and wonders; and other valuable principles. $6.95

Could You Not Tarry One Hour?
by Larry Lea

To many Christians prayer is a drudgery. Larry Lea
has discovered that prayer can be a pleasure and
we can learn how to enjoy it. The more we learn
to "tarry one hour," the more we will grow in
likeness to Christ and the more we will be able
to bring His timeless message to a world in pain.

$12.95

ISBN 0-88419-198-2   Hardback

Riding the Wind
Your Life in the Holy Spirit
by Everett (Terry) L. Fullam

Raise your sails and let the gentle breezes of the
Holy Spirit move in your life. Learn more about
Him and His availability to you in this personal
and biblical book by one of America's finest
teachers. $7.95

ISBN 0-88419-196-6   Trade Paper

Available at your Christian bookstore or from:

190 N. Westmonte Drive
Altamonte Springs, FL 32714
(305) 869-5005